*Gloria
Patri*

Gloria Patri

The History and Theology
of the Lesser Doxology

NICHOLAS AYO, C.S.C.

University of Notre Dame Press
Notre Dame, Indiana

Designed by Wendy McMillen
Set in 11.7/14 Pavane by Four Star Books
Printed on 55# Nature's Recycle Paper in the U.S.A. by Versa Press

Library of Congress Cataloging-in-Publication Data

Ayo, Nicholas.
    Gloria Patri : the history and theology of the lesser doxology /
Nicholas Ayo.
        p.   cm.
    Includes bibliographical references.
    ISBN-13: 978-0-268-02029-3 (pbk. : alk. paper)
    ISBN-10: 0-268-02029-9 (pbk. : alk. paper)
    1. Gloria Patri.   2. Doxology—History and criticism.   I. Title.
    BV194.D69A96   2007
    242'.72--dc22

                                                    2007019521

To Richard Downs, C.S.C.,

who ever spoke to everyone of the glory of the Blessed Trinity and of our future glory in the sight of God.

Contents

PART TWO.   *The Trinity in Time and Eternity*

Preface

In this book I intend to explore a short, familiar, but little reflected upon prayer—the "Glory to the Father and to the Son and
to the Holy Spirit, as it was in the beginning, is now, and will be
forever." Along with the Lord's Prayer and the Hail Mary, the so-
called lesser doxology[1] may be the most recited prayer in Christian devotion.

Comprising the first three chapters, part one will give back-
ground and foundation—linguistic, theological, and historical—
for understanding the lesser doxology as a prayer. In the first chapter I will introduce doxology as a recognition of the mystery of
God. In the second chapter I will explain what the first word of
the Gloria Patri implies. Amply understood, "glory" (to God) contains the whole prayer. A linguistic analysis of the Greek word
doxa, which in English is rendered "glory," will be given. A theological explanation of glory will complement the verbal analysis. In the third chapter I will outline the history of the lesser doxology. I will explain how it has been elaborated and modified in
its wording and its usage in the liturgy throughout the centuries
from the beginnings of Christianity.

Comprising the remaining chapters, part two will further examine the prayer itself, phrase by phrase and word by word. In the fourth chapter, the meaning of the Trinitarian address to God is considered at length. The next several chapters consider separately the past, the present, and the future, that is, "in the beginning, is now, and will be forever." These time frames amplify the comprehensive perspective of this succinct yet profound Christian prayer.

The lesser doxology deserves examination word by word because it is a concentration of prayer that compresses in a few words a rich theology. Many scholars believe that the prayer life of the Church undergirds the theology of the Church, much as the faith itself supports the theology that seeks to understand it. The so-called *lex orandi, lex credendi*[2] presumes that spirituality and theology are related and entwined, and to study one while oblivious of the other may well cause a distortion. Hence there is a meditative quality to the examination of this prayer that presumes a meditative context for its recitation. My audience is not neatly divided between scholars, who need not be believers, and believers, who need not be scholars. Theology proceeds at its peril when divorced from Church life. Most theologians would affirm that conclusion. In this brief book about a short but pivotal Christian prayer, I hope to show how theological examination can enrich praying, and how the Gloria Patri, inviting spiritual reflection, can ground and deepen a theology of glory.

Acknowledgments

Many people have generously assisted me in this endeavor. Nathan Mitchell gave me the breadth and depth of his wisdom in matters liturgical, and he responded to many questions, offered various suggestions, and read the manuscript at various stages and in its totality with a critical eye and generous heart. Eleanor Bernstein, C.S.J., and the resources of the Center for Pastoral Liturgy at the University of Notre Dame were ever helpful, and their annual conferences inspirational as well as informative. Fr. Herman Reith, C.S.C., a former teacher and mentor of mine in my undergraduate days, suggested the idea and gave me the encouragement to undertake this topic. Jeff Gainey at the University of Notre Dame Press not only guided me through the many tasks involved in publication, but he also read the manuscript more than once and gave substantive suggestions for its emendation and improvement. Matt Dowd, also with the press, suggested many improvements in clarity and arrangement. I thank Susan Pusztai for permission to use her "A Poem of Glory." Fr. James Burtchaell, C.S.C., gave me my initial introduction and lifelong love of liturgy some fifty years ago. The support of the members of the Congregation of Holy Cross, as well as the faculty and students of the Program of Liberal Studies and the University of Notre Dame, is so constant as to be unnoticed, but it is not taken for granted. I remain grateful and beholden to all these people and others unmentioned, whose contributions I may have forgotten or overlooked. "No man is an island" is a wisdom well understood by authors.

The Lesser Doxology

Glory to the Father and to the Son and to the Holy Spirit,
as it was in the beginning, is now, and will be forever. Amen.

Post-Vatican II version

Glory be to the Father and to the Son and to the Holy Spirit,
as it was in the beginning, is now, and ever shall be,
world without end. Amen.

Pre-Vatican II version

The Greater Doxology

Glory to God in the highest and peace to his people on earth.
Lord God, heavenly king, almighty God and Father.
We worship you, we give you thanks, we praise you for your glory.
Lord Jesus Christ, only Son of the Father. Lord God, lamb of God,
you take away the sin of the world. Have mercy on us.
You are seated at the right hand of the Father, receive our prayer.
For you alone are the holy one, you alone are the Lord,
you alone are the most high, Jesus Christ, with the Holy Spirit,
in the glory of God the Father. Amen.

PART ONE

Doxology: Word and Concept

Doxology as Mystery of God

Doxology is the most exalted verbal expression and the climactic liturgical gesture of the assembled community of faith. Doxology is a formula of praise always dedicated to God and God alone. Doxology is the moment of greatest intensity in prayer. Failing in our own words, we readily acknowledge that only the very Word of God can give perfect glory to God. "Long ago God spoke to our ancestors in many and various ways by the prophets, but in these last days he has spoken to us by a Son, whom he appointed heir of all things, through whom he also created the world. He is the reflection of God's glory and the exact imprint of God's very being, and he sustains all things by his powerful word" (Heb 1:1–3).[1] Only God can speak adequately of God. Jesus is our Word of God and hence our ultimate doxology. Our prayer to the Father is always through the Word and in the unity brought about among us by the Holy Spirit. As the Eucharistic Prayer concludes in its own great doxology: "Through him, with him, and in him in the unity of the Holy Spirit, all glory and honor is yours, almighty Father, for ever and ever. Amen."

In the context of worship services, the word "doxology" refers specifically to a short formula of thanksgiving and glory given to God at the closing of a longer prayer formulation. Doxologies can be found throughout the Hebrew and the Christian scriptures. Doxological prefaces to prayers and more often conclusions were common in the Jewish synagogue. The early Christians continued the practice of doxologies, but the formulations now confessed Jesus Christ as Lord. Early in Christian worship, for example, in the second-century *Didache,* we find this doxology added to the Lord's Prayer: "For thine is the kingdom and the power and the glory, forever. Amen." So widespread and popular was this doxology that the words themselves were copied into some ancient Bible texts and for centuries were thought to be originally from Matthew's gospel. In the eastern Church, liturgical prayers commonly ended with a doxology. In the western Church, the liturgical recitation of individual psalms commonly ended with a doxology. In classical Christian preaching in the Patristic age, homilies often ended with a doxological formula.[2] Eventually the Trinity—Father, Son, and Holy Spirit—in all their mystery and ultimate divine glory became the heart of all Christian doxology.

The psalms are filled with praise and worship of God, and for that reason they remain a prime example of doxology in the Jewish faith. Each of the five books of the Jewish Psalter concludes with a doxology in praise of the one true God. Book I ends "Blessed be the Lord, the God of Israel, from everlasting to everlasting. Amen and Amen" (41:13). Book II concludes, "Blessed be the Lord, the God of Israel, who alone does wondrous things. Blessed be his glorious name forever; may his glory fill the whole earth. Amen and Amen." (72:18–19). Book III ends "Blessed be the Lord forever. Amen and Amen" (89:52). Book IV concludes, "Blessed be the Lord, the God of Israel, from everlasting to everlasting. And let all the people say, 'Amen.' Praise the Lord!" (106:48). And the last book of the Psalter concludes with Psalm 150, which in its entirety is a doxology. The psalms were appropriated by Christians and given a particular Christian interpretation by the general practice of ending the liturgical recitation of each psalm with the lesser doxology.

Doxology in the Christian liturgy clearly took its lead from doxology in the Bible. The epistles of Paul are peppered with doxological prayers and especially laudatory salutations at the beginning of epistles and praise excitations at their conclusions. "For from him and through him and to him are all things. To him be the glory forever. Amen" (Rom 11:36), and Paul concludes his Epistle to the Romans "to the only wise God, through Jesus Christ, to whom be glory forever! Amen" (Rom 16:27). Paul writes in the beginning of Ephesians: "Blessed be the God and Father of Our Lord Jesus Christ, who has blessed us in Christ with every spiritual blessing in the heavenly places, just as he chose us in Christ before the foundation of the world, to be holy and blameless before him in love" (Eph 1:3–4). And later in the same epistle: "Now to him who by the power at work within us is able to accomplish abundantly far more than all we can ask or imagine, to him be glory in the Church and in Christ Jesus to all generations, forever and ever. Amen" (Eph 3:20–21). And we read in Philippians: "To our God and Father be glory for ever and ever. Amen" (Phil 4:20).

Turning to the gospels, the so-called greater doxology, the Gloria in Excelsis of the Eucharistic liturgy, is an amplification and elaboration of the angels' praise and glory revealed to the shepherds at the birth of Jesus in Bethlehem. "Glory to God in the highest heaven, and on earth peace among those whom he favors!" (Lk 2:14).[3] Mary's Magnificat in Luke's gospel (1:47–55) echoes Hannah's hymn of praise in the first book of Samuel (2:1–10). The lesser doxology, the Gloria Patri that is the subject of this book, developed from Christian faith in the Trinity, which has beginnings in a text such as the baptismal formula at the conclusion of Matthew's gospel: "Go therefore and make disciples of all nations, baptizing them in the name of the Father and of the Son and of the Holy Spirit, and teaching them to obey everything that I have commanded you. And remember, I am with you always, to the end of the age" (Mt 28:19).

The First Letter of Peter contains the doxology later appended to the Lord's Prayer in its liturgical recitation: "To him belong the glory and the power forever and ever. Amen" (1 Pt 4:11). And this same epistle concludes: "And after you have suffered a little while, the God of all grace, who has called you to his eternal glory in Christ, will himself restore, support, strengthen and establish you. To him be the power forever and ever. Amen" (1 Pt 5: 10). The last book of the Bible is adorned with lyrical doxologies, such as: "To the one seated on the throne and to the Lamb be blessing and honor and glory and might forever and ever!" (Rev 5:13) and "Amen! Blessing and glory and wisdom and thanksgiving and honor and power and might be to our God forever and ever! Amen" (Rev 7:12).

The gradual development of a Trinitarian formula used in the liturgy as part of many prayers can be established. "The Martyrdom of Saint Polycarp" in the second century displays the Trinitarian formula: "I bless Thee [Lord God, Almighty Father], through the eternal and heavenly High Priest, Jesus Christ, Thy beloved Son, through whom be to Thee with Him and the Holy Spirit glory, now and for all the ages to come. Amen."[4] The "Canon of Hippolytus" in the third century reads: "In each prayer which is said over each thing, there is said at the end of the prayer, Glory to you, Father, Son, and Holy Spirit, to the ages of ages."[5] Origen writes: "And having begun by glorifying God it is fitting to conclude and bring the prayer to an end by glorifying him, hymning and glorifying the Father of the universe through Jesus Christ in the Holy Spirit, 'to whom be the glory for ever' (Rom 16:27)."[6] Clement of Alexandria concludes his extended homily on the rich man in the gospel story with a clear and elaborate Trinitarian doxology addressed to the "Pater ille, qui est in coelis, . . . cui cum Filio Jesu Christo, qui vivorum et mortuorum

Dominus est, per Spiritum Sanctum, fit gloria, honor, potestas, aeterna majestas, nunc et semper, et in generationes generationum, inque secula seculorum. Amen." In English, "To the Father, who is in heaven . . . who with the Son, Jesus Christ, who is Lord of the living and the dead, through the Holy Spirit, be glory, honor, power, eternal majesty, now and forever, from generations to generations and from ages to ages. Amen."[7]

In the ancient creeds in their tripartite structure, Father, Son, and Holy Spirit are clearly professed. The *Te Deum* remains a magnificent and ancient doxology surpassed by none. Doxology in the East remains even more entrenched than in the West. Jungmann writes "In the Byzantine liturgy, most *orationes* begin with the address 'Lord our God' and end: '(For thou art a good and merciful God and) to thee we send up praise, to the Father and to the Son and to the Holy Spirit, now and always and to all eternity. Amen.'"[8]

Christian hymns follow the practice of Christian prayers. There are many doxologies that conclude sacred songs, but none as felicitous as Bishop Ken's memorable verses sung to the tune of the "Old Hundredth": "Praise God from whom all blessings flow, / Praise God all creatures here below. / Praise God above ye heavenly host, / Praise Father, Son, and Holy Ghost." The *Tantum Ergo* of Eucharistic devotion ends with a magnificent doxology: "Genitori, Genitoque / Laus et jubilatio, / Salus, honor, virtus quoque / Sit et benedictio; / Procedenti ab utroque / Compar sit laudatio." In English, "To the one begetting and to the one begotten [the Father and the Son] may there be praise and jubilation, together with welfare, honor, and power, along with blessing; and to the one who proceeds from them both [the Holy Spirit] may there be like adoration."

The spiritual impact of doxology in Christian prayer should not be overlooked. Given there is a God, and if that God is for us and we are truly the beloved of God, how can we not also rejoice in the being of God in all its glory? Our doxology is not directed to a God who would collect our applause. Our doxology is our recognition of the truth, the wonderful reality of our creation and salvation, and our invitation to dance with God for eternity in friendship and love. Doxology is praise, praise that changes not God but us. We awake. We recognize the beauty and goodness of the infinite God.[9] We look into the kaleidoscope of God's marvelous works, and we are changed from despair to overwhelming hope that "if God is for us, who is against us?" (Rom 8:31). Liturgy is always about the recognition of what God is doing and our giving thanks "always and everywhere." Doxology is the heavenly prayer, the prayer of endless awe and admiration, the prayer that acknowledges we have nothing without the boundless mercy of God and everything with God's grace. And of that we are assured. Glory be to God!

The Philology and Theology of Glory

The Philology of Glory

The translation of the Latin *gloria* into the English glory is straightforward and requires little comment. Glory in English will, of course, carry connotations that may vary from time to time and place to place. Living languages change; usage changes; dictionary meanings change in the futile attempt to stay current in the wonderful world of human language in all its creative manifestations.[10]

Living faith also creates meaning by its practice of praying. The *lex orandi, lex credendi* (the rule of prayer is the rule of belief) reflects this truth. Believers pray first, and then reflect on their expressed faith. People live the faith first, and theology follows to record practice, much like people talk and write first, and the dictionary follows to understand usage. Living faith and living language both manifest the wonderful creativity with words that allows for new meanings that reflect new realities. We shall see below how this principle that life precedes codification plays out with the word "glory." The way believers used the word glory led to new definitions, and these in turn led to a particular understanding of the word glory in all its glory.

Hebrew Glory

In the Hebrew Scriptures the "glory of God" is rendered by *kebod YHWH*.[11] In its profane meanings, *kabod* suggested "(1) weight or burden, (2) riches or wealth, (3) importance, and (4) prestige, renown, honor (royal prestige, majesty)."[12] In the earliest biblical understanding, the glory of God was seen in the theophanies of nature. "The heavens are telling the glory of God" (Ps 19:1). Especially in storm lightning and thunder was the glory of the Lord revealed. "The voice of the Lord is over the waters; the god of glory thunders" (Ps 29:3). Moses on the top of Mt. Sinai witnessed a great theophany of the Lord God: "Now the appearance of the glory of the LORD was like a devouring fire on top of the mountain in the sight of the people of Israel" (Ex 24:17). In one account Moses is given to see the face of God, and afterward he veiled his own face to protect onlookers from the reflected radiance of God (Ex 34:29–35). In another account, Moses is given to see only the back of God as the divinity passes by in glory (Ex 33:20–23). Vermeulen writes: "The *Kebod Yahveh* is primarily the concrete Divine Being in so far [as] This reveals Itself to man, and secondarily stands for the more or less abstract divine attributes connected with the appearance of this divine Being, notably the refulgent splendour of God, His might and Majesty."[13]

In the Mosaic revelation, the "glory of the LORD filled the tabernacle" with a cloud by day and fire by night (Ex 40:34–38). That glory of God was a presence through thick and thin as Israel wandered in the desert in search of the Promised Land. As the glory of God became less phenomenal in its portrayal, a new word was coined by Jewish commentators on the Hebrew Scriptures. *Shekinah* suggested the tenting of God or the indwelling of God, and emphasized the on-going presence of God with God's people. God's glory was not necessarily overwhelming as the storm, though it ever remained awesome. From the glory of God in the heavens to the glory of God in the Temple was a journey of human understanding. The greater reality was found in the deliberate presence of God and not in the boundless power of God. In his vision of the glory of God that fills the Temple, Isaiah writes: "Holy, holy, holy is the LORD of hosts; the whole earth is full of his glory" (Is 6:3). Ezekiel, the "prophet of the glory of God" writes eloquently of his many visions of the glory of the Lord that filled the Temple (see Ez 1, 10, and 43 in particular). The *shekinah* became the source and center of the Lord God's glory. *Kebod YHWH,* however, was not replaced so much as it was enhanced.

Greek Glory

When the Hebrew Scriptures were translated into Greek (the *Septuagint* composed in the second century B.C.), the Hebrew word *kabod* was rendered throughout with the Greek word *dóxa.* Vermeulen argues that *epiphaneia* (in English, epiphany) "would undoubtedly have been a more adequate rendering of *Kabod.*"[14] *Epiphaneia* seems to have been rejected because of its pagan religious connotations going back to the theophanies in the writings of Homer. It was a word also used to describe the divinization of emperors and princes.[15]

Dóxa in the Greek Bible is commonly rendered in English as "glory."[16] The term "doxology" is composed of two words: *dóxa* and *logos. Logos* is a word for word itself or for mind (reason). Thus biology is the reason or words about life (*bios*). A great deal has been written of the Christianization of *logos,* a word with multiple meanings in Platonic and Neoplatonic philosophy. As Christians began to use *logos* to speak of the Word of God, who is the Son of God and our Lord Jesus Christ, the connotations of *logos* became more theological than philosophical.[17] But the transition was gradual and at times confused. The shift of *dóxa* as used in classical Greek to *dóxa* as employed in Christian theology and liturgy over the first centuries of Christianity also makes for a story of complexity marked by gradual development. Christine Mohrmann claims that the choice of the Greek *dóxa* to translate the Hebrew *kabod* was a radical and extraordinary shift of meaning.[18] Thus the word doxology comes to us transfigured from classical Greek into a Christian theology that grew out of Christian faith and practice. Doxology would be translated well as "word of glory," or "praise." "Worship" would also not be an implausible synonym.

The Hebrew word *kabod* was a quite common word for glory. *Kabod* has a root meaning of weighty. One's *kabod* signifies all that one amounts to, one's weight in the world, both possessions and reputation. One's *figura* might capture that idea of *kabod* as *dóxa,* and *dóxa* as glory. The Latin *claritas, majestas, gloria,* and *honor* were more or less captured by the Greek *dóxa,* but it was a stretch to convert *dóxa* into the glory of God. To comprehend and render verbally what the glory of God entails seems no easier today. Of the weight of glory, C. S. Lewis writes: "To please God . . . to be a real ingredient in the divine happiness . . . to be loved by God, not merely pitied, but delighted in as an artist delights in his work or a father in a son—it seems impossible, a weight or burden of glory which our thoughts can hardly sustain. But so it is."[19]

Laurentin outlines the theological development of the word *dóxa* through the first four centuries of Christianity, beginning with *dóxa* understood as power and deed, to *dóxa* understood as origin and source, and finally to *dóxa* comprehended as the divine essence.[20] Vermeulen summarizes his study of *dóxa* in the Bible: "we may say that both in the Old and the New Testament, *dóxa Theou* stands for (1) the refulgent appearance of God, or His shining power and greatness; (2) the eschatological—in the New Testament even the anticipated—participation of man in God's greatness."[21]

The roots of the Greek word *dóxa* contain some useful implications. Before the Christian era, *dóxa* referred to the opinion or judgment that a person might profess. If one's opinion proved wise, one was thought to be orthodox, that is, a person of right (*ortho*) judgment (*dóxa*). If one appeared wise in the eyes of others, one's *dóxa* was all the more worthy. In the Christian era *dóxa* became associated with the divinity. Since reputation formed one's abiding glory, whose fame could outdo the fame of God? Hence *dóxa* became the word fitting the divine glory spoken of God and spoken to God. In the end *dóxa* never lost a link to its ancestry as opinion, but opinion that was far more than the typical Greek understanding of the appearance of being glorious. *Dóxa* developed into the Christian proclamation of the hidden knowledge of the very nature of God, who now is glory itself, and of humanity, which in mystery shares God's glory.

Because *dóxa* implies fame, rightly deserved fame or reputation becomes one's glory. Orthodoxy means right fame, rightly deserved reputation. Doxology might then be understood as words about getting it right. Doxology becomes simply the way things are. Doxology is the truth of the human condition before God. Doxology is the plain truth. God is glorious, and God's ways are glorious for human beings, who are made in the image of God. In the end we become doxology, and our lives are "words" of glory to God. "The glory of God is the salvation of the world. Doxology and soteriology are one theologically"[22] The Church thus gives glory to God in the work of human salvation with an unending cascade of doxologies.

Roman Glory

"The glory that was Greece and the grandeur that was Rome."[23] Cicero defined Roman *gloria* as *frequens de aliquo fama cum laude*[24] (enduring and praiseworthy personal reputation). Augustine defined *gloria* as *clara cum laude notitia*[25] (manifest display of praise). *Dóxa* in the Greek Christian scriptures was translated into Latin with the word *gloria.* In the Old Latin versions prior to Jerome's vastly influential *Vulgate* translation, *dóxa* was sometimes translated by *claritas,* which captured the rich imagery of light that was lost in the word *gloria.*[26] *Majestas* is also found, but eventually *gloria* dominated the Latin Bible. The word was not originally a happy choice, for it came with connotations of worldly empire. *Gloria* was the ancient world's hope of immortality; the grave was the end, only fame endured. The change of *gloria* from the word appropriate for Roman military victory and a divinized political power in the figure of the Roman emperor remains the story of how Christian usage led to Christian redefinition. Glory that began as renown in the eyes of human history became glory in the eyes of God's eternity. The military glory of the Roman general was replaced by the spiritual glory of the Christian martyr. The utter shame of the crucified criminal became the very glory of God revealed in the Son of God who rose from the dead. The glory of this world was overshadowed by the glory of the Kingdom of God. The glory of the earth became the glory of heaven, and the glory of the divinized Emperor, the glory of the Lord Jesus. Perhaps a way to understand the baptism of words in Christian usage is to recall the Christianization of the Roman winter festival of the return of the sun: the celebration of Christmas on the darkest day of the year glorifies the Son of God made flesh, who is now the true light of the world. *Lex orandi, lex credendi* is well illustrated in this one word *glory,* which was transfigured from the very pagan connotation of the emperor as God to the exaltation of Jesus Christ as the King of kings and the true King of Glory.

The Theology of Glory

God's glory is from within. By the free act of creation, God gains nothing and enjoys no further glory. God's glory is infinite already, was forever, and will be forever. Eternity is beyond time. Let us reflect upon the nature of God as fully God and established forever in infinite glory. God is simple because only an infinity that is everything can claim there is nothing other. God does not pursue truth: God is Truth. God does not seek beauty: God is Beauty. God does not have glory: God is Glory. The only and one God has been revealed to us to be Father, Son, and Holy Spirit. Therefore, Father, Son, and Holy Spirit is/are Glory. The mystery of God is a mystery of glory. "In the doctrine of the Trinity and in Christology *gloria* comes to designate the divine nature proper to the Father, the Son and the Spirit."[27]

Given God's full and perfect glory, which cannot be enhanced nor demeaned by any created glory, human beings should never be envisioned as servants whose work provides more glory to God. God does not need us to do God's work, though God allows us to do what is God's work. Although we are co-creators with God, pro-creators in the work of giving life, God's will at its depth is not designed to make us servants but to make us friends. God, of course, needs neither friends nor servants, but God chose us to be friends, and friends must be free. There can be no friendship without freedom. Therefore God wants each human being to do what at their deepest and truest selves they choose to do, that is, to be truly themselves. That maturation of God's gift of creation reveals the glory of God. "So, whether you eat or drink, or whatever you do, do everything for the glory of God" (1 Cor 10:31). C. S. Lewis speaks well of this glory in us: "Next to the Blessed Sacrament itself, your neighbor is the holiest object presented to your senses. If he is your Christian neighbor, he is holy in almost the same way, for in him also Christ *vere latitat* [truly is hidden] — the glorifier and the glorified, Glory Himself, is truly hidden."[28]

God surely wants us to be human, and only that, but human fully and deeply as revealed and realized only in the humanity of Jesus Christ. God wants finally not the human nature of an Apollo but the humanity of his beloved son, Jesus our Lord, whose graced humanity we had never imagined. That graced humanity, which is ours in the gift of the Holy Spirit in the depths of every human being's heart, wishes to lay down its life for its friends. Such sacrifice stems not from duty, command, or guilt, but out of the truest self-identity and out of the fullest free love welling up from the gift that is our very being, made in the image of God who is love. In that kaleidoscope of humanity radiant in love with every color appears God's glory. C. S. Lewis writes of fidelity to God's gift of freedom: "when human souls have become as perfect in voluntary obedience as the inanimate creation is in its lifeless obedience, then they will put on its glory, or rather that greater glory of which Nature is only the first sketch."[29] St. Irenaeus concludes succinctly: *Gloria Dei vivens homo* (a vital human being is the glory of God).[30] And his words but echo St John: "My Father is glorified by this, that you bear much fruit and become my disciples. As the Father has loved me, so I have loved you; abide in my love" (Jn 15:8–9). The Jesuit motto, *Ad Majorem Dei Gloriam* (For the Greater Glory of God), is not the aphorism of an indebted servant, but rather the response of a beloved friend of God who eschews self-glorification in this life for the God-intended self-fulfillment that is found in living for God. "Let your light shine before men, so that they may see your good works and give glory to your Father in heaven" (Mt 5:16). Our glory is God's glory and God's glory is ours.

In the end, creation and redemption kiss. *Kabod* as the glory of creation and *shekinah* as the abiding presence of God dovetail. Doxology as praise of God and soteriology as the salvation of God join hands. Communicating divine life to the world establishes God's glory among us. A "universe totally transfigured by the glory of God, receiving glory from Him and rendering glory to Him"[31] manifests a divine reciprocity that in creaturely fashion reflects the very life of the Trinity, in which the divine being of God is totally exchanged in an eternal communion that gives itself and receives itself in endless love.

If the Father has "loved them [us] even as you [the Father] have loved me [Jesus]" (Jn 17:23) then we also are the beloved sons (and daughters) of God. Jesus says "the glory that you [the Father] have given me I have given them" (Jn 17:22). Thus when we say the doxology, "Glory to the Father and to the Son and to the Holy Spirit," we pray with Jesus within the mystery of the Trinity indwelling in our hearts. We truly are the adopted and graced children of God and the sisters and brothers of Jesus our Lord. The doxology, therefore, is not only a statement about the Trinity and an acknowledgment of how glorious it must be to be God. The doxology enacts and embodies our inclusion in the glory of God, that "they may be one, as we [Father and Son] are one, I in them and you in me, that they may become completely one, so that the world may know that you have sent me and have loved them even as you have loved me" (Jn 17:22 – 23). When one ponders the great discourse at the last supper in John's gospel (chapters 13 – 17) one may well understand why the mystics write of the love of God as a marriage between humanity and divinity.

We receive in our very existence a participation in the divine glory that is the life of God, and we return that glory in our praise and worship. "Yet for us there is one God, the Father, from whom are all things and for whom we exist, and one Lord, Jesus Christ, through whom are all things and through whom we exist" (1 Cor 8:6). As the Son receives the glory of being God from the Father and returns it perfectly to the Father in the Holy Spirit, so we human beings are included in a created way in this mystery of exchange of the Trinitarian life. "See what love the Father has given us, that we should be called children of God; and that is what we are. . . . Beloved, we are God's children now; what we will be has not yet been revealed. What we do know is this: when he is revealed, we will be like him, for we will see him as he is" (1 Jn 3:1 – 2).

As we have seen above, the meaning between *claritas* and *gloria* overlaps. The glory of God is manifest in the beginning of creation: "Let there be Light!" Moses on top of Mt. Sinai saw the flames of YHWH, the same flames he saw at the burning bush, when the Lord said: "I AM WHO I AM" (Ex 3:14). Zechariah sings of the coming light: "By the tender mercy of our God, the dawn from on high will break upon us, to give light to those who sit in darkness and the shadow of death" (Lk 1:78–79). On top of Mt. Tabor the face of Jesus "shone like the sun, and his clothes became dazzling white" (Mt 17:2). Paul is struck down on the road to Damascus by a great light, and he hears a voice from heaven saying, "Saul, Saul, why do you persecute me?" (Acts 9:4). Dante in his *Paradiso* consummates his vision of God as a white rose of pure light (Canto 31). Thoreau concludes *Walden* with the promise that tomorrow holds ever so much more light than today: "The sun is but a morning star." We know God as light. We await the beatific vision, when we will be able to look upon the sun/Son of God with eyes open to infinite splendor. We shall then see not only the three primary colors of our human creation, but an infinite array of divine colors never seen on earth. We await the new Jerusalem coming down from heaven like a bride dazzling in the beauty of her sparkling jewels. "And the city has no need of sun or moon to shine on it, for the glory of God is its light, and its lamp is the Lamb" (Rev 21:23). "And the fire and the rose are one."[32]

The History of the
Gloria Patri Doxology

Paul gives us the earliest Christian scriptures, and his greeting might well be the text most succinctly supportive of the Christian invocation of the Trinity, which is prayed today at the beginning of the Eucharistic liturgy: "The grace of the Lord Jesus Christ, the love of God, and the communion of the Holy Spirit be with all of you" (2 Cor 13:13). Such a claim need not imply that Paul elaborated a theology of the Trinity. From the beginning, Christians were trying to comprehend the mystery of God as revealed in Jesus Christ and as known through the gift of the Holy Spirit within the human heart.

The gospel contains the testimony of Jesus himself to the Father and the Holy Spirit. No more than of Jesus than of Paul need we claim an elaborate theology of the Trinity. Clearly Jesus called God his Father (*Abba*). Clearly Christians came to believe, in light of the resurrection experience pondered deeply, that Jesus was Lord God. And clearly Jesus promised to send the Holy Spirit, whom Christians would receive at Pentecost. That Holy Spirit changed hearts from hard to soft, from hateful to loving. Such a miracle of forgiveness only God could accomplish. Thus Christians first experienced the mystery of God through the works of God—the mediation of Jesus and the descent of the Holy Spirit. Prayer was directed to the Father through Jesus and in the Holy Spirit. In the preconciliar era, the Holy Spirit was understood not so much as the third person of the Trinity but rather as the grace of God received in the Church assembly. Christian prayer developed from Christian experience, and lived faith and prayer prompted further theological questions of depth and complexity. The practice of prayer became the inspiration of theology, and the development of theology shaped the later composition of prayers.

The Gloria Patri is composed of a statement, "Glory to the Father and to the Son and to the Holy Spirit" and a comparison, a simile to be exact, "as it was in the beginning, is now, and will be forever, [world without end]." The Trinitarian statement of the first part is the older part. It owes its final verbal formulation to the disputes over the divinity of Jesus that would eventually culminate in the Arian controversy dealt with at the Council of Nicaea (325) and at the Council of Constantinople (381) and resolved succinctly in the Nicene Creed we recite to this day. It is to this historical formulation embodied in the lesser doxology that we now turn.

In the early Church there were many baptismal creeds. Not much centralization was possible in the beginning, and local churches composed creeds according to their faith and understanding—creeds buttressed by oral tradition and later by written gospels, but tailored to the time and place. Indeed, the creeds are older than the gospels, for the profession of faith and the rite of baptism could not be postponed. One lived the faith before one wrote its scriptures. The doxologies enjoyed the same kind of free development. Prayers in Christian liturgy typically ended with a formula of praise of God, much as Jewish prayers, which were held as models, concluded. Controversy in the Church gave rise to later standardization both in creed and in doxology. Prayer and theology developed side by side in mutual interaction: first one leading, then the other. Still, one lived and prayed before one reflected and put words into careful composition. Both creed and doxology were intentionally profound icons of prayer and worship, and only subsequently did they become touchstones of orthodoxy.

The Apostles' Creed developed out of an even earlier Roman creed, and it gradually became popular and adopted in areas beyond Rome itself. The Nicene Creed, a creed fashioned not so much out of liturgical practice as out of conciliar debate in time of doctrinal struggles in the Church, became a creed of exact wording designed to separate orthodox belief from error in the faith. The Arian controversy, which pitted belief in Jesus as God's greatest creation versus belief in Jesus as "one in being" with the Father, sparked rigorous wording (for example, setting on the word *homoousion* to describe "one in being") of the orthodox creed at the Council of Nicaea. A similar struggle fifty years later at the Council of Constantinople (381) established that the Holy Spirit likewise was to be adored and glorified together with the Father and the Son. With the Niceno-Constantinopolitan creed (popularly called the Nicene creed), the one God in three divine persons, the Blessed Trinity of catholic faith, was clearly and universally proclaimed. It would be a long time before that reality would be always and everywhere confirmed.

Almost nothing in the formulation of Christian prayer is as simple in examination as it is in appearance. "Glory to the Father through the Son and in the Holy Spirit" was frequently the preferred composition of the doxology that developed as the Christian elaboration of the Jewish doxology, "Blessed be the Lord God." In the early Church, and particularly in the East, collects of liturgical prayer typically concluded in Trinitarian fashion: "we ask this through our Lord Jesus Christ, your Son, who lives and reigns with you and the Holy Spirit, one God, for ever and ever." The complication in this otherwise simple and straight-forward piety stemmed from a possible reading of Jesus as mediator subordinate in some way to the Father. The Arian controversy racked the Church with divisive controversy beyond imagining because of the political and theological divisions swirling around whatever side of this question was adopted. Was Jesus a demigod, but the greatest of God's creation? Was he nonetheless a creature dependent upon the one God, the Father almighty? Or was Jesus, whose humanity was created and dependent, nonetheless equal to the Father, "light from light, true God from true God, one in being" with the Father? Paradoxically, one needs to remember that within the economy of salvation there remain traces of subordination that is not the Arian heresy, but rather the way the incarnate God has come to humanity. The Son of God receives his being from the Father, which while not implying inequality does suggest a "source" and a direction.

In Basil the Great's small treatise "On the Holy Spirit,"[33] the wording of the lesser doxology occupies a large part of his text. His concern was to establish the full and glorious divinity of the Holy Spirit, but that celebratory affirmation became entangled with disputes about the orthodox wording of the Trinitarian doxology typically used to conclude Christian prayer. In the Syriac liturgy of the Eastern Church and environs, the wording developed in the following fashion. "Glory to the Father with (*méta*) the Son together with (*sún*) the Holy Spirit," according to the Greek rendition. In the Greek-speaking liturgies of the East, however, the wording was customarily "Glory to the Father through (*dìa*) the Son and in (*én*) the Holy Spirit." Basil wanted to use both versions of the doxology. He argued that "through the Son and in the Holy Spirit" brought out the economy of salvation strongly in its suggestion of the redemptive role of Jesus and the ongoing sanctification of the Church by the Holy Spirit. Basil also wished to keep the wording "with the Son together with the Holy Spirit," which he thought underlined the worshipful praise of the communal Trinity. Thus, the preposition "with" maintained the mutuality of the three divine persons of the Trinity while still emphasizing the equality.

Basil hoped this ancient formulation would oppose and correct the Arian subordinationist reading of "through the Son and in the Holy Spirit." Unfortunately, he was accused of unwarranted innovation in the liturgy. The wording of the doxology became a war of prepositions and a red herring in the divisive arguments and civil strife within factions of the one Church. Basil was then harshly accused of using wordings that could be understood as Arian subordination of the Son and Spirit. The pervasive Arian atmosphere generated an abrasive orthodox atmosphere. Listen to Basil himself describe his times and his struggles in his superb fourth-century treatise:

> They fight against each other with harsh words; they nearly fill the church with the meaningless cries and unintelligible shouts of their incessant clamor. They continually pervert the teachings of true religion, sometimes by adding to them, and other times by reducing them. On the one hand are those who confuse the Persons and revert to Judaism; on the other are those who oppose the natures, and are swept away into Greek polytheism. Inspired scripture is powerless to mediate between these two parties, nor can apostolic tradition offer them terms of reconciliation. One honest word and your friendship with them is finished; one disagreement with their opinions is sufficient pretext for a quarrel. No oath is so effective for holding a conspiracy together as common fellowship in error. Every man is a theologian; it does not matter that his soul is covered with more blemishes than can be counted. The result is that these innovators find an abundance of men to join their factions. So ambitious,

self-elected men divide the government of the churches among themselves, and reject the authority of the Holy Spirit.[34]

The orthodox theology that recognized Father, Son, and Holy Spirit as three equal and divine persons in the Holy Trinity, one God, acknowledged that the wording of the lesser doxology was open to an Arian interpretation. "To the Father through (*dìa*) the Son and in (*én*) the Holy Spirit" gave a very descriptive account of how humanity received salvation through the Son and how appropriately humanity might return in the Holy Spirit its prayers of praise and thanksgiving to God. The equally ancient formulation well known in the Syrian liturgy, "To the Father with (*méta*) the Son together with (*sún*) the Holy Spirit," emphasized the communal nature of the Godhead more directly, but it also did not underscore equality of being.[35] Any formulation that did not use the coordinate conjunctions "and (*kai*) to the Son and (*kai*) to the Holy Spirit" was thought to deal in Trinitarian modalities and not realities.

"Glory to the Father *and* to the Son *and* to the Holy Spirit" thus became the new orthodoxy, patterned on the tripartite creed that proclaimed belief in the Father and the Son and the Holy Spirit quite separately and deliberately. The war of the prepositions was engaged. The sad but poignant account of its widespread bitterness is recounted at length in Basil's treatise:

I have explained the force of both expressions [preposition or conjunction]. Now I shall again describe their similarities and differences in usage. They are not antagonistic expressions; it is simply that each has a unique meaning, as far as true religion is concerned. The preposition *in* expresses the relationship between ourselves and the Spirit, while *with* proclaims the communion of the Spirit with God. Therefore we use both words: the

latter expresses the Spirit's dignity, while the former de-
scribes the grace we have been given. We glorify God
both in the Spirit and with the Spirit; we have not in-
vented this word, but we follow the teaching of the Lord
as our rule, and transfer this word to things which are
logically related, sharing a common mystery: He is num-
bered *with* Them in the baptismal formula, and we consider it necessary to combine Their Names in the same
way when we profess our faith, and we treat the profession of faith as the origin and mother of the doxology.
What can they do now? Either they must teach us not to
baptize in the manner we have been taught, or else not
to believe as we were baptized, or not to glorify as we
believe. Can anyone deny that the sequence of relationship in these acts must necessarily remain unbroken?
Will anyone deny that innovation here will mean disas-
ter everywhere? Still they continue screaming in our ears
that to give glory *with* the Holy Spirit is unauthorized,
unscriptural, et cetera. We have already said that as far
as our understanding is concerned, to say "Glory to the
Father *and* to the Son *and* to the Holy Spirit" means the
same as "Glory to the Father *and* to the Son *with* the Holy
Spirit." We have received the word *and* from the very
words of the Lord, and no one would dare to deny or can-
cel it, so what could possibly hinder our acceptance of
its equivalent? We have already shown the similarities
and differences between the two words. Our argument
is confirmed by the fact that the Apostle uses both words
indifferently: he says in one place "in the name of Our
Lord Jesus Christ *and* in the Spirit of our God" and in
another "When you are assembled and my Spirit is present *with* the power of our Lord Jesus." He obviously has
no idea that using the conjunction or the preposition
affects the combination of names in any way.[36]

The Gloria Patri thus places all three divine persons on a level of equality separated only by coordinating conjunctions. As Basil points out, there is a biblical warrant for the coordinate conjunctions "and/and" in the conclusion of Matthew's gospel, "baptizing them in the name of the Father *and* of the Son *and* of the Holy Spirit" (Mt 28:19). One needs to remember, however, that the "and/and" in Matthew is hardly the developed Trinitarian theology of the divinity of the Son (Nicaea) and the divinity of the Holy Spirit (Constantinople), even though it stands not in opposition to the later, more developed theology of the Trinity.

Basil noted that scripture supported "with/with" even if not in so many words, but Basil accepted the "and/and" wording as a way to end the bitter dispute. The lesser doxology as recited today in the Catholic Church follows a wording accepted in the Church in large measure because of the irenic spirit of Basil the Great, who was willing to compromise on a wording he thought unnecessary, even if quite acceptable all around.

While the Gloria Patri today in popular use can be attributed to the peace that Basil struck in the compromise wording of the Gloria Patri that seemed to satisfy all the disputants in the war of prepositions, we can see that the richness of a variety of doxological expression was not lost in the Church. Collects in the Eucharistic liturgy of the West, and in the Divine Office as well, typically conclude with an ending rich in the connotations of the economy of salvation, which Basil was eager to employ in his public prayer: "We ask this through Our Lord Jesus Christ, your Son, who lives and reigns with you and the Holy Spirit, one God, for ever and ever." Most of the collects in the Latin liturgies adopt a formulation of "through the Son and in the Holy Spirit" because it addresses so well the incarnation of the Son of God and his continued mediation in the gift of the Holy Spirit, who is the soul of the Church. We can also see something of this inspiration in the formulation of the greater doxology, the "Glory to God in the Highest," and especially in the great doxology at the end of the eucharistic prayer: "Through him, with him, and in him, in the unity of the Holy Spirit, all honor and glory are yours almighty Father for ever and ever. Amen."

In sum, the "and/and" that coordinate the three persons of the Trinity is clearly found in the Christian scriptures in the Matthean baptismal formula, even though a developed Trinitarian theology was probably not intended by the evangelist. The "with/with" or the "through/in" that encompasses the persons of the Trinity in relation to the economy of salvation in which grace comes through Jesus Christ and in the Holy Spirit is not found so readily in the gospel scriptures, but reflects an early theology developed by Paul. We need not end the war of the prepositions with an either/or resolution. The mystery of God is immense and boundless, and all doxology but approaches the ineffable divinity with great humility. Both/and, which allows us to have the doxology both ways, is the peace suited to the *mysterium tremendum*. Indeed we have much to treasure in the several doxologies. Each in its own way captures a distinct color of God's overwhelming light. In the end, the lesser doxology remains a magnificent confession of faith and of praise of God from whom all blessings flow, the one God of mystery—the Father, and the Son, and the Holy Spirit.

Post-Patristic Developments

The doxology we are studying has roots in the early centuries of Christianity. Herbert Thurston claims: "After the Our Father, it may be fairly held that the *Gloria Patri* affords the earliest example of an ancient Christian prayer which is still in every day use."[37] The wording of this traditional prayer, however, has occasioned much dispute. We have examined above the first part of the doxology, the "Glory to the Father *and* to the Son *and* to the Holy Spirit." In the selection of the prepositions in the Greek doxology that preceded the Latin and the adoption eventually of the coordinating conjunctions "and/and," we do witness a doctrinal struggle, with the doxology as a lightning rod in a much larger issue concerning the divinity of the three persons of the Trinity. Similarly, in the second part of the lesser doxology, there remains disputed wording. Both at the beginning, "as it was in the beginning," and at the ending, "world without end," the text has not been universally accepted.

John Cassian witnesses to the late fourth-century practice of saying the lesser doxology at the close of each psalm in the Divine Office.[38] The sixth-century *Rule* of Benedict also speaks clearly of the lesser doxology as a way to punctuate and to Christianize the recitation of the psalms by the regular repetition of the Trinitarian doxology.[39] The second half of the lesser doxology probably was shaped as a response in the alternating liturgical recitation of the psalms. The first part of the doxology was answered in the antiphonal choir with the second part. Part two of the lesser doxology echoes, with variation, part one. The typical parallelism of the psalms was thus given to the doxology itself. The comparisons (was/is/will be) were meant to echo and amplify the original statement, "Glory to the Father and to the Son and to the Holy Spirit."

The oldest refrain to Trinitarian praise was simply "for ever" or "for ever and ever. Amen." Somewhat later the text was expanded to read "now and for ever." The "now" did not add new meaning but made temporal expectations more explicit, leading to phrases such as "now and ever" or "now and forever." In short, "Glory to the Father . . ." always. The ending of the Ave Maria, "now and at the hour of our death," has a similar structure. The intent is to secure Mary's intercession always, from beginning to ending. "Unto ages of ages" was often added at the very end of the doxology as a further echo of "now and forever." The established doxological text in Greek makes this clear: *Dóxa Patri kai Uiôi kai hagiô Pneumati* kai nun *kai aei kai eis tous aiônas tôn aiônôn. Amên.* The English translation could be easily lined up with the Greek words: "Glory to the Father and to the Son and to the Holy Spirit, *both now* and forever and unto ages of ages. Amen."

To the second half of the lesser doxology, which originally was quite brief, a small prologue was added. That clause, "As it was in the beginning" (*sicut erat in principio*), is found, however, only in the Latin. The additional text seems to have been introduced as a late refutation of the Arian heresy, one of whose pivotal claims asserted that there was a time when the Word of God (who was made flesh) was not, in other words, that the Son of God was created in time as the perfect creature but had not existed from the beginning (from all eternity beyond time). The intention of Arianism was to preserve the one and only God, and if the Word of God were divine it would seem there were two Gods. As we will see below, it is not perfectly clear how the addition of this text refuted once and for all the Arian claim, since a beginning even from all eternity raises the whole issue of dependency and the creation of time *ex nihilo.* The "beginning" was usually understood, however, as a paraphrase of "from all eternity," the way God always was (note how we cannot talk of eternity without words taken from our human time frames).

The Council of Vaison, in the Province of Avignon (Arles) in southern France, in the year 529 issued this decree in Canon V: *Et quia non solum in sede apostolica, sed etiam per totum Orientem, et totam Africam, vel Italiam, propter haereticorum astutiam, qui Dei Filium non semper cum Patre fuisse, sed a tempore coepisse blasphemant, in omnibus clausulis post* Gloria, Sicut erat in principio *dicitur, etiam et nos in universis ecclesiis nostris hoc ita dicendum decernimus.*[40] In English: "Because not only in the Apostolic See [Rome], but also throughout the East and in all Africa and Italy, in all the concluding words following the *Glory be* there is said *as it was in the beginning,* we judge that in all our Churches this formula must be so said, on account of the cunning of the heretics [Arians] who blaspheme in holding the Son was not always with the Father but to have a beginning in time" (translation mine). The Council of Toledo in 633 (presided over by St. Isidore of Seville) reinforced the decree of Vaison and also ratified once again the recitation of the doxology at the end of the liturgical recitation of each psalm.[41]

The Council of Vaison was wrong about the inclusion of the "as it was in the beginning" in the East, where it was never adopted. In fact, the Greeks reproached the Latins about the addition of the *sicut erat in principio.*[42] In truth, the text had been included in the lesser doxology in the West from well before the sixth century and Vaison, and eventually it was adopted everywhere in the West except in the Mozarabic liturgical rite in Spain, which reads: "Glory and honor be to the Father and to the Son and to the Holy Ghost, world without end [unto ages of ages].[43]

We have seen how the coordinate conjunctions "and/and" in the baptismal formula at the end of Matthew's gospel (28:19) were used as a warrant for the "Glory to the Father *and* to the Son *and* to the Holy Spirit." Similarly one can find a biblical warrant for "as it was in the beginning": the opening line of the prologue to John's gospel, "In the beginning was the Word," serves well, for the thrust of John's text is precisely to establish the divinity of the Word of God from all eternity, even though the Word became flesh and dwelt among us in a particular time and place.

The various translations into English of the Latin *sicut erat in principio et nunc et semper et in saecula saeculorum. Amen* have caused considerable controversy. *The Book of Common Prayer,* sponsored in the sixteenth century by Henry VIII after his separation from the Roman Catholic Church, has been the standard English translation almost everywhere in the English-speaking countries of the world until after the second Vatican Council. "Glory be to the Father and to the Son and to the Holy Spirit, as it was in the beginning, is now, and ever shall be, world without end." Today we find a revised wording in the Roman Catholic liturgy: "Glory [be] to the Father and to the Son and to the Holy Spirit, as it was in the beginning, is now, and will be for ever [and ever shall be, world without end]. Amen."

One difficulty some persons have with either English liturgical translations above stems from the verbs. In Latin, there is only the past tense verb *erat* (was), even though *et nunc* (now) *et semper* (and forever) imply a present tense verb with *nunc* (is now) and a future tense with *semper* (will be forever). Some Latin texts read not *et nunc et semper* but *est nunc* (is now) *et semper,* which may have been a corruption of the text driven by a reading that insists upon the insertion of verbs in the verbless Latin text. And, it should be noted, the "world without end" (a free translation of *in saecula saeculorum*) has been omitted altogether in the contemporary Roman Catholic liturgical version.

Sicut erat in principio, et nunc et semper raises further questions of translation into English. *Et* following *sicut* is typically rendered as *so,* just as *kai* following *ôs* in Greek is translated as *so.* Thus we should read "as [it] was in the beginning, so now, and for ever." Several other similar wordings have been offered in a protracted correspondence in *The Tablet* over the years (1884, 1901, and 1913), such as: "May glory be given to the Father . . . now and for ever, such as was given in the beginning." Or, "as in the beginning so in the world without ending." Or, "Glory be . . . now and for evermore, even as it was in the beginning."

In the Lord's prayer we see the same construction: *Fiat voluntas tua, sicut in coelo et in terra.* The translation in English reads: "Thy will be done on earth *as* it is in heaven." If the *sicut/et* in the *Pater Noster* were translated as the *Book of Common Prayer* translates the *sicut/et* of the doxology, the Lord's Prayer would read "Thy will be done as it is in heaven and it is on earth." What is at stake is this: we do not wish to equate the will of God as done in heaven (well) and now on earth (not well), we want the will of God well done on earth as it is well done in heaven. Similarly, we do not settle for glory to God as it was in the beginning (well given) and is now (not well given), etc. We might want to say "as this glory of God was well given in the beginning, so now may it be well given and forever." In the Divine Office for the feast of the Most Holy Trinity, the antiphon for

First Vespers reveals a Latin construction similar to the lesser doxology: *Gloria Tibi Trinitas, aequalis, una Deitas et ante omnia saecula, et nunc et in perpetuum.*" In English, "Glory to you Trinity, all equal, one Divinity, as before all ages *so now* and forever" (translation mine). One might understand either "so [it is] now," or "so [may it be] now." The issue is not easily resolved.

Let us look at translations of the lesser doxology in other modern languages. A typical German translation of the Latin favors reading the Latin *et* as *so:* "Wie im Anfang, so jetzt und in Ewigkeit" (As in the beginning, so now and forever). A typical French translation of the Latin agrees with the German: "Gloire au Père, et au Fils, et au Saint-Esprit: maintenant et toujours, comme dès le commencement et dans les siècles des siècles." (Glory . . . now and always, as [so] from the beginning and unto ages of ages).[44] Or in a variant on the French: "Gloire soit au Père . . . et qu'elle soit telle aujourd'hui, et toujours, et dans les siècles des siècles, qu'elle a été dès le commencement et dans toute l'éternité." (Glory . . . may it be such today, and always, and unto ages of ages, as it has been from the beginning and through all eternity).[45]

An Old English translation of the fourteenth century, before Henry VIII and the *Book of Common Prayer* reads: "as it was in the bygyning and now and ever and into the worldis of worldis. So be it."[46] John Dowden reports that "more than a hundred years later, in the Primer of 1535, we read: 'As it was in the beginning, as it is now, and ever shall be. So be it.' Here we have (a) the verb repeated and the tense altered, so as to suit the adverbs of time; and (b) the difficult 'in saecula saeculorum' silently skipped."[47] In the King's Primer of 1545, probably the work of Cranmer, we read: "As it was in the beginning, and is now, and ever shall be, world without end. Amen."[48] This text with its ambiguities actually prevailed to this day and became the text of the accepted *Book of Common Prayer* through the subsequent centuries. Later texts render the Latin *sicut . . . et* in various ways. For example, a sixteenth-century text reads: "As it was in the begynninge as it is now and ever shall be."[49] An eighteenth-century text reads: "As it was in the beginning, so be it now, and for ever, world without end."[50] In sum, does one want to emphasize the eternal glory of God, as it is now, or to emphasize the human reflection of God's glory, would that it may be now?

The original wording of the doxology in a translation of the Greek, without the precautionary addition of the *sicut erat* in the Latin, reads as follows: "Glory to the Father and to the Son and to the Holy Spirit, so now and forever." There are no verbs. Accordingly *sicut erat in principio,* a later gloss on the original doxological text, should be read as a parenthesis and as an anti-Arian addendum. Thus the reading that could prevail when all is said and done might preserve both of the readings explored above: "Glory to the Father and to the Son and to the Holy Spirit, so now and forever (as in the beginning)." One might also place the parenthesis first: "(As in the beginning) so now and forever."

The matter of *sicut erat* is yet more complicated. Whether or not one reads it as translated in the *Book of Common Prayer* or relocates it as a parenthetical addition either at the beginning or closing of the second part of the lesser doxology, the verb *erat* has no determined subject. A subject in the Latin is only implied. Why do we translate into English with the pronoun "it," which the Latin does not require? The anti-Arian thrust of this clause was surely to say "as he (the Son) was in the beginning." Some modern language translations even say just that, for example, "als er [he] war im Anfang." If we ignore "he" and insist on "it," what is the antecedent of the "it"? As the Trinity was in the beginning? As the glory was in the beginning? As "world without end[ing]" was in the beginning? As the case may be—a generic "it"—in the beginning? All the above? One might also argue that were the subject for *erat* not *gloria* but rather the Trinity itself—Father, Son and Holy Spirit—the "as it was in the beginning, is now, and will be forever" with equal mood in the verb tenses would seem a more unobjectionable translation.

Let us complicate matters even more. Establishing the mood of the implied verbs of the doxology is a matter that determines how one reads this prayer. One commentator on the English translation in the *Book of Common Prayer* argues for the implied verbs to be construed in the imperative mood. He laments a "loss of force in the aspiration, from the substitution of the indicative for the imperative form; as the object surely is to *join* in all this glory, which arises in all time, to light it up, as it were, in the centuries and make it our own, not from the beginning only, but time out of mind, without beginning and without end."[51]

Three renditions of the lesser doxology are plausible depending upon the chosen or given mood of the verb "to be." In the indicative mood, the words read in effect: "Glory . . . as it was in the beginning, is now, and will be forever." The doxology is a statement and the liturgical English translation, whether the approved translation now used in the liturgy or its predecessor as found in the *Book of Common Prayer* over the centuries, is an accurate and straightforward translation of the Latin. As a statement of fact—glory is given to the Trinity, together with a prophecy that glory will be given in the future as it was in the past. The indicative mood of the verb presents no ambiguity: one stands in time—past, present, and future, and thus the lesser doxology becomes a confession of faith. Vermeulen argues that *gloria* came to mean in both theology and in liturgy the divine nature proper to the three divine persons. Consequently, "The doxology receives an entirely new and anti-Arian signification. St. Ambrose uses it at the end of every sermon. . . . In the doxology he always uses the indicative. Especially the short doxology, *Gloria Patri et Filio et Spiritui sancto* comes to designate the acknowledgment of the unity of the divine nature and the three divine Persons."[52]

If one prefers, however, to read the doxology as a prayer of petition, a desire to see God glorified in the three persons of the Trinity and for all time, past, present, and future, then the verb belongs in the optative mood. "(May) glory be to the Father . . .

as it was in the beginning, so be it now and forever." Jungmann writes: "The later, pure Trinitarian doxology is probably always to be taken as subjunctive, as we, in fact, are accustomed to understand it: Glory *be* to the Father."[53]

If one reads the doxology as neither statement primarily, nor petition, but rather as a prayer of praise, an exclamation of the Blessed Trinity, then the verb would belong in the imperative mood. One could even omit the verb, as the old Greek version did, thus "Glory to the Father . . . now and forever." Accordingly the doxology is not a declaration of fact, nor a plea that praise be given, but is itself praise to God: "What we really do is: We *give* glory in the same way in which it *has been* given, *is* given, and *shall be* given for all eternity."[54] One stands in eternity couched in terms of time, rather than standing in time couched in terms of eternity.

One might think of *blessing* as illustrative of this use of the imperative mood. The "Divine Praises" are just such a doxology in the imperative: "Blessed be God, Blessed be his Holy Name" etc. The doxology at the end of the Canticle of Daniel, which is said regularly at Sunday morning prayer in the Divine Office, catches the tone of the Gloria Patri: "Let us bless the Father and the Son and the Holy Spirit. Let us praise and exalt him forever. Blessed are you, Lord, in the firmament of heaven. Praiseworthy and glorious and exalted above all for ever."

The verbs in the doxology are only implied. The *sicut erat* remains a didactic parenthesis and not the controlling tense or mood for the whole doxology. Read with verbs in indicative mood, the doxology becomes an eloquent confession of faith in the eternal Trinity. Read with verbs in the optative mood, the doxology becomes a soulful petition for the glorious exaltation due God's being. Read with verbs in the imperative mood, the doxology becomes an acclamation and a cry of the heart enthralled by the living God. In the end one need not decide among the three plausible moods of the verb implied in the lesser doxology. None of the readings following one mood or the other is wrong or unworthy of being affirmed devoutly. In all likelihood, even all three moods capture only in a limited way the essence of doxology, that quintessential praise of God for being God, who is recognized as such by humanity in awe and in wonder.

Post–Vatican II English Translations

In *Prayers We Have in Common* (1970 and 1975) sponsored by the International Consultation on English Texts (ICET), the text was rendered without verbs. Thus, "as in the beginning, so now, and for ever." However, the text without the verbs of the second part (was, is, will be) proved to be unsatisfactory, particularly in hymnody. Hence in *Praying Together: A Revision of "Prayers We Have in Common,"* the text was changed to include the implied verbs.[55] In the *Catholic Household Blessings and Prayers* approved for the United States, the English translation of the lesser doxology follows a revised text of the ICET: "Glory to the Father and to the Son and to the Holy Spirit: as it was in the beginning, is now, and will be forever. Amen." That text represents what is found in the Divine Office in its revision following the second Vatican Council.

The English version found in the *Book of Common Prayer* reads, "ever shall be, *world without end.*" "Will be forever" seems a parallel rendering of "ever shall be," but what happened to "world without end"? The sense of these last words may seem redundant, but they are clearly found in the Latin text of the doxology, in use in the Roman liturgy for centuries. *Gloria Patri et Filio et Spiritu Sancto, sicut erat in principio et nunc et semper et in saecula saeculorum.* If one omits the *sicut erat in principio,* the doxology in the Greek reads exactly as the Latin. Both Greek and Latin conclude with "world without end," *et in saecula saeculorum.* The Vatican Instruction, "Liturgicam Authenticam," (issued in April of 2001), which outlines principles for the vernacular translation of liturgical texts, may result in a restoration of a literal English translation of the Latin text and the inclusion again of the familiar "world without end." Perhaps an even more accurate and felicitous translation of the Latin will emerge.

At the conclusion of prayers from early Greek liturgy to the present day the phrase *eis tous aiônas tôn aiônôn* is pervasive. The Greek word *aiôn* is the dominant root word, rendered in late Latin as *aeôn*. The English derivative of the Greek and Latin is "eon." Westcottt defines the plural of *aiôn, (aiônes)* as "the sum of the periods of time including all that is manifested in and through them."[56] The ecclesial Latin preferred *saeculum* as the translation of *aeôn*. Thus in the plural *in saecula saeculorum* would be well translated into English as "unto the ages of ages" or in the "in the eons of eons." "World without end" is the translation in the *Book of Common Prayer,* and while it does not give a literal translation of the Latin or Greek, it certainly does address the meaning of eon, defined in the *American Heritage Dictionary* as "an indefinitely long period of time, an age, eternity." Pre-Reformation translations from the Latin were more literal and used an old Anglo-Saxon meaning of world as a period of time. "Glory be to the father, and to the son, and to the holy goost. As hyt was yn the begynnyng, so now, and euer, and yn the world off worlds."[57] Or "Glorie be to the fadir and to the sone and to the hooli goost. As it was in the begynning and now and euermove and in to the worldis of worldis."[58]

There is a biblical warrant for the phrase "unto the ages of ages." It is found in the Hebrew scriptures. For example, David prays in the following manner: "Blessed art you, O Lord, the God of our ancestor Israel, *forever and ever*" (1 Chr 29:10). Daniel prays in similar manner: "Blessed be the name of God *from age to age,* for wisdom and power are his" (Dan 2:20). And in the psalms we pray "Blessed be the Lord, the God of Israel, *from everlasting to everlasting.* And let all the people say, 'Amen.' Praise the Lord!" (Ps 106:48).

The "ages of ages" phrasing is also found in Christian scriptures. The Greek word *aiôn* occurs more than one hundred times with a meaning of [for] ever or eternity or age. In the Epistle to the Galatians we read: "Our God and Father, to whom be the glory *forever and ever*. Amen" (Gal 1:5). And again "To our God and Father be glory *forever and ever*. Amen" (Phil 4:20). In the First Letter to Timothy we read, "To the King of the ages, immortal, invisible, the only God, be honor and glory *forever and ever*" (1 Tm 1:17). And in the Second Letter to Timothy: "To him be the glory *forever and ever*. Amen" (2 Tm 4:18). In the Epistle to the Hebrews the author concludes "through Jesus Christ, to whom be glory *forever and ever*. Amen" (Heb 13:21). In the First Letter of Peter we find the same formulation addressed to Jesus Christ: "To him belong the glory and the power *forever and ever*. Amen" (1 Pt 4:11; and see also 5:11). Matthew's gospel concludes "I am with you always, to the end of the age" (Mt 28:20). The "end of the age" seems an echo of "I am with you always," just as in the doxology "world without end" echoes "ever shall be" (or "will be forever"). More than one example can be found in the Book of Revelation, such as "to the one seated on the throne and to the Lamb be blessing and honor and glory and might *for ever and ever!*" (Rev 5:13) and "Amen! Blessing and glory and wisdom and thanksgiving and honor and power and might be to our God *forever and ever!* Amen" (Rev 7:12).

Another explanation of the seemingly redundant Latin version of the lesser doxology may stem from Jewish prayer practice. In the Mishna (Berakoth 9) one may note an expansion of the usual "for ever" conclusion of the Benedictions: "But when the Sadducees perverted their ways and asserted that there was only one world, it was ordained that the response should be 'for ever and ever,'" an ending that the Sadducees intended as the extension of time in this world without any known end, rather than a reference to an eternity, in which they did not believe. One might argue that the Christian doxologies took over the verbal ending of the Jewish prayer practice and gave it an orthodox Christian meaning that encompassed eternity.

It seems unclear exactly why "world without end" has been dropped from the liturgical text now in use in the English translation. Granted "world without end" is not a literal translation of *in saecula saeculorum,* which is admittedly hard to translate into idiomatic English. Moreover, the text may seem redundant, since "will be forever" carries a similar import. It may be that for public recitation or public song, the longer text is at issue. Nonetheless, I lament the loss of a bit of elegant poetry that goes back in Christian prayer tradition to the very earliest times, and which has roots in the Bible as well. All things considered, I would prefer in liturgical prayer that we would keep "world without end-[ing]" or an alternative translation such as "unto the ages of ages" or "forever and ever," which would be acceptable translations of the Greek and the Latin, respectively. Not only does this concluding phrase continue an unbroken tradition, the text underlines the glory of God for all eternity *in the ending,* which gives a bookend closure to "as it was *in the beginning.*"

If I were asked to suggest a translation of the lesser doxology, I would offer this English version and for the following reasons: "*Glory to the Father and to the Son and to the Holy Spirit, as in the beginning so now and always, for ever and ever.*" I drop the one verb in the Latin (*erat*) and I do not specify the implied verb that belongs to the statement part (the first part) of the doxology. The implied verb, if construed in the subjunctive or optative mood would make the doxology a prayer or brief oration, in other words (would that) glory be given to the Father, to the Son and to the Holy Spirit as it (glory) always was, is, and will be. If construed in the indicative, however, the implied verb would make a quasi-creedal proclamation: glory (understood as the very being of God) is (ascribed) to the Father, and to the Son, and to the Holy Spirit as it (the very being of God) was, is, and will be. Thus in a verbless version the issue of the mood of the verb may be resolved in multiple and complementary ways. Without "it" the question of the antecedent is also resolved in favor of multiple meanings. "For ever and ever" is a more compelling translation than "world without end" of the Greek *aiônas tôn aiônôn* in the phrase "unto ages of ages" (literally "unto eon of eons") and of the Latin *in saecula saeculorum* in the phrase "unto worlds of worlds." "For ever and ever" has a musical tone, and the preceding word, "always," (*semper* in the Latin) includes not only eternal time but also suggests all ways, or infinite activity, in an eternity that is not static but dynamic.

The Course of Development

Let us summarize. If one were asked to give an account of the Gloria Patri in its genesis, one should begin with the recognition that prayer itself as the expression of faith is the engine that powers theology. People first lived the faith and prayed the faith before they thought about it in a systematic way or came to write about it at length. Precisely prayer to the Father through the Son and in the Holy Spirit was a prayer that reflected how people came to faith. Jesus was the revelation of the Father, and Jesus was known in the Holy Spirit in the Church. Such prayer gave rise to theology, and the Arian heresy was a deficient theology that rose out of that same gestalt. The persons of the Trinity seemed so in contradiction to the one and only transcendent God of Judaism that one would be surprised if the Arian quandary had not captured the minds of so many. The Arian controversy went to the very heart of Christianity. No other threat risked the very essence of Christianity. "Who do you say I am?" is the question that Jesus asks in the gospel of his disciples, and the question continues to be asked to this day. If Jesus is but a creature, however great, Christianity remains a version of Judaism. Only when Jesus is seen as fully both human and divine does the essence of Christianity emerge.

Not only does prayer generate theology, but theology generates prayer. The so-called *lex orandi, lex credendi* (the rule of prayer is the rule of belief) cuts both ways. Our behavior affects our thought, but our thought affects our behavior as well. Usage determines the dictionary definition, but dictionaries in turn modify usage. As a fuller theology of three divine persons in one God began to prevail, the doxology, under some pressure to combat Arianism, moved to the coordinate "and/and" of the current text: "Glory to the Father *and* to the Son *and* to the Holy Spirit." Thurston argues that "the earliest clear example of the form, 'Glory to the Father *and* the Son *and* to the Holy Ghost'" occurs in the fourth-century "De Virginitate" of Athanasius, which reads "Glory to the Father and to the Son and to the Holy Spirit, both now and forever and into the ages."[59] And it was Athanasius who stood against the world in the Council of Nicaea when the Arian dispute was resolved. Jungmann summarizes the historical import of the Arian controversy in these words: "Granted that the Arian assault had not changed the faith of the ancient Church, yet it has profoundly influenced, at first throughout the East, the use made of different facets of the faith in the religious and liturgical life."[60]

A similar phenomenon can be noted with the development of the creeds. The Apostles' Creed, originally a baptismal confession, does not deny anything of the doctrine of the Trinity if read generously and sympathetically. It is open to various theological interpretations, however, because of the imprecision of its language. The Niceno-Constantinopolitan Creed, a conciliar creed worked out at the Council of Nicaea (325) and of Constantinople (381), makes the theology of the Trinity precise and explicit and beyond all interpretation that wished to preserve the one and only God at the expense of the divine persons of the Trinity.

If the first half of the doxology was formed in dialogue with the historical and theological issues facing the early Church, the second half in its earliest form owes more to function than to controversy. "Now and forever" is the substance of the text. "Is now and will be forever" is an elegant way of saying "always." Glory to God (Father, Son, and Holy Spirit) always. "Unto ages of ages," which is a quite literal translation of the concluding phrase in the Greek and Latin, may seem a redundancy, but it is an elegant way of saying "forever and ever" (always and always). "As it was in the beginning" proves to be a later parenthesis, easily placed at the beginning of the line or at the end.[61] The phrase is not found in the Greek, which is the basis for the Latin text in all the other words of the doxology. "As it was in the beginning" should be judged a late western addition to the doxology, designed to counteract the Arian slogan that there was a time in the beginning when the Word of God did not yet exist and hence must have been created by the one infinite God.

The development of the second half of the doxology, as we mentioned above, probably stemmed from the recitation of the doxology in public liturgical prayer at the end of each psalm of the morning and evening prayers of the Church. Thus the doxology offered a parallel construction much like what is frequently found in the psalms themselves. Nothing essential is added to the first part of the doxology by the inclusion of the second part, although it does elaborate the mystery of time and eternity. Thus we have a rough parallel and a deliberate echo. In sum, the two-part doxology yields two evenly balanced lines suitable for choral recitation as well as private prayer.[62] The doxology in both parts enjoyed biblical support and also provided poetic amplitude. Prayer was thus married to doctrine.

PART TWO

The Trinity in Time and Eternity

"Father, Son, and Holy Spirit"

The lesser doxology proclaims glory to God as "Father, Son, and Holy Spirit." What understanding of the Trinity might one bring to this prayer and its spiritual implications? In short, how does prayer addressed to the persons of the Trinity enhance the lesser doxology?

In the beginning God created humankind as the apex of creation. Male and female he created them, and in the image of God were human beings made. "Let us make humankind in our image, according to our likeness" (Gen 1:26). The plural "us" may well be the royal plural of the heavenly court in the biblical writer's metaphorical resources, but Christians have seen an allusion to the Father, Son, and Holy Spirit. Accordingly, each and every human being is created in the image of the triune God, who is the full revelation of the one God. What might that mean for us? Jesus tells Mary Magdalene that he is about to ascend "to my Father and your Father, to my God and your God" (Jn 20:17). When human beings prepare themselves, they are capable of entering into the very intimate personal life of God. We are called to be created participants in the infinite relationship and boundless

45

exchange of "knowledge and love" that is the essential life of the one and only God, "Our Father who art in heaven."

Human beings can befriend their pets, but they can never hope for a true conversation with them. Our animals are not made in the image of human beings. But we human beings are made in the image of God, and we have been given a capacity to be raised up to spiritual friendship with God in a "world without end." Such a creation is the very glory of God in this world, and we are the recipients and the reflection of that spatial glory of God manifest in time. "I will greatly rejoice in the Lord, my soul shall exult in God; for he has clothed me with the garments of salvation, he has covered me with the robe of righteousness, as a bridegroom decks himself with a garland, and as a bride adorns herself with her jewels" (Is 61:10).

In the mystery of the Son of God made man, we human beings have been elevated to become the adopted sons and daughters of God. In Jesus Christ we maximize what was only incipient in our creation in the image of God. In our Lord Jesus we have become by God's gracious and gratuitous choice the very adopted daughters and sons of the Father. We are promised the resurrection of our bodies and a place with Jesus who sits at the right hand of the Father in glory.

In his epistles Paul did not claim an articulate theology of the Trinity. Such a theology came much later with the first ecumenical councils in the fourth century. Neither would Paul have disregarded the further development of his thought. He knew the revelation of the Trinity even without precise words, much as a child knows parental love even before the child can speak. Living faith always precedes the words of a consequent theology, as living language precedes the work of the lexicographer.

Trinity: Mysterium tremendum

Whole bookshelves are written about the Trinity,[1] and these books agree among themselves mostly about the ineffable mystery that is the blessed Trinity. As in a Japanese garden where less is more, I hope to arrange a few carefully chosen words of the many reflections by many authors upon the mystery of the Trinity. All believers know that the divinity they speak of remains unspeakable, ever surpassing human understanding. Consequently, my few words about the Trinity will not pretend to say what cannot be said, even in many words.

We already know something of God because of the revelation of creation, which revelation culminates in the human life of the Lord Jesus Christ. Classical theology proclaims the mystery of the Trinity in its fullest human revelation "'brought about' by that Spirit—consubstantial with the Father and the Son—who, in the absolute mystery of the Triune God, is the Person-love, the uncreated gift, who is the eternal source of every gift that comes from God in the order of creation, the direct principle and, in a certain sense, the subject of God's self-communication in the order of grace. The *mystery of the Incarnation constitutes the climax* of this giving, this divine self-communication."[2] What Christians know of the revealed mystery of the triune God stems from the incarnation of the Son of God and the indwelling of the Holy Spirit of God in the people of God. The sacramental words of penance recapitulate the saving intent of the Trinity: "God the Father of mercies through the death and resurrection of his Son has reconciled the world to himself and sent the Holy Spirit among us for the forgiveness of sins. Through the ministry of the Church may God give you pardon and peace, and I absolve you from your sins in the name of the Father and of the Son and of the Holy Spirit." We have no other window into the intimate life of God. There is no God hidden in eternity that is not revealed, albeit imperfectly and in faith, in the work of creation, salvation, and sanctification that provides our knowledge of the Trinity in time. Because action follows being, one might argue that the life of the Trinity in this world follows in some way the life of the Trinity that is identical with the being of the Trinity. "God for us is who God is as God."[3] The glory of God implicates the Trinity in its life of self-sharing in time with the Trinity in its life of self-sharing in eternity. "There is only one God, one self-communication, one triune mystery of love and communion, which has both eternal and temporal modalities."[4]

Jesus prayed to his Father, *Abba* (Mk 14:36), and taught us to pray "Our Father in heaven" (Mt 6:9). Jesus who is Lord, however, was not talking to himself. The Father and the Son were revealed to us. And Jesus promised to send the Holy Spirit, who would forgive our sins (Jn 20:22–23) in the changing of our hearts as only God could do. The earliest gospel baptismal formula we have comes with Trinitarian implications: "baptizing them in the name of the Father and of the Son and of the Holy Spirit" (Mt 28:19).[5] Human beings are made in the image of God. If God is a Trinity, then human beings are made in the image of the Trinity. By the same logic, the work of creation, the work of redemption, and the work of sanctification are made in the image of God who is Father, Son, and Holy Spirit at every turn. "The doctrine of the Trinity pertains to the ecstasy of God in its eternal and temporal dimensions."[6] That reciprocity, however analogous, between the manifestations of God in time and the very essence of God in eternity as the one and only God—Father, Son, and Holy Spirit— remains the *mysterium tremendum.*

Gloria Patri: Trinitarian Invocation

The doxology we are examining has two parts. The first part concerns glory to the three divine persons of the Trinity. "Father and Son and Holy Spirit" are separated by coordinating conjunctions in a grammar that reinforces the equality of persons in the theology. The second part of the doxology concerns the past, the present, and the future. "As it was in the beginning, is now, and ever will be" extends the action of the triune God throughout time and implies eternity. "To reflect on the mystery of the triune God is to reflect on events past, present, and future that disclose the mystery of God who is pure and unbounded love. In this sense, theological reflection on any aspect of the mystery of redemption in Christ can legitimately be regarded as Trinitarian."[7] The first part of the doxology is revealed to us in the second part, because the love of God from all eternity is shared according to the very being of the triune God in created-out-of-nothing time— past, present, and future. The concern will be *"to give glory to the Trinity,* from whom everything in the world and in history comes and to whom everything returns."[8] And again, Christ "embraces within his redemptive power *the whole past history* of the human race, beginning with the first Adam. The *future* also belongs to him: 'Jesus Christ is the same yesterday and today and for ever' (Heb 13:8)."[9]

Whatever one person of the Trinity does, God does, for there is only one God. Thus it is not exact to say the Father creates, the Son redeems, and the Holy Spirit sanctifies the world. The Son and the Holy Spirit also create the world, and the Father also is saving, and the Holy Spirit as well, for there is only one God. Only the Son of God became flesh, yet the Son of God is truly the one God. The generation of the Son by the Father is not unrelated to the generation of the world in creation, however, nor unrelated to the incarnation of the Son in redemption. Though the divine persons are distinct, their activity is the activity of the one God. "Creation is the work of the Triune God. The world 'created' in the Word-Son, is 'restored' together with the Son to the Father, through that Uncreated Gift, the Holy Spirit, consubstantial with both. In this way the world is created in that Love, which is the Spirit of the Father and of the Son. This universe embraced by eternal Love begins to exist in the instant chosen by the Trinity as the beginning of time"[10]

We are accustomed to think that Jesus Christ gave his life for humankind. And that is true indeed. But Jesus also died out of love for his Father, who gave his Son to us out of love for us and out of love for his Son, now manifest in time as the Father's love for us. Thus the life of God in eternity and the life of God in time are mysteriously conflated. God in God's self and God in this world are mirror images, assuming we allow for the unspeakable gap between the uncreated and the created. Thus "the doctrine of the Trinity is not ultimately a teaching about 'God' but a teaching about *God's life with us and our life with each other. It is the life of communion and indwelling, God in us, we in God, all of us in each other.*"[11]

The Son of God is begotton of God the Father. The Son is not created, but eternally generated from the being (essence or substance) of the Father, "because you [Father] loved me before the foundation of the world" (Jn 17:24). The conciliar term coined at Nicaea — *homoousios,* the same being/substance with the Father — proclaimed Jesus to be Lord God. From the Father every reality stems. It is the Father's infinite immensity that accounts for all existence. Source of sources, love of all loves, the prodigality of the Father of mercies overflows into the necessary love of the Father and the Son and the Holy Spirit, and into the unnecessary (contingent) but prodigal love that is all of creation, redemption, and sanctification, culminating in the Beatific Vision of such unsurpassable privilege promised humanity in heaven.

The "big bang" hypothesis for the material genesis of the universe compares but little with the internal ecstasy of love that implodes in the infinite Trinity of persons in an eternally loving reciprocity. Perhaps only the agony of the crucified Jesus gives a glimpse of the uncontainable extravagance of the love of the Father reflected in the equal love of the Son in the mutual love of the Holy Spirit. And we are created in the image of God, the triune God. And we are made in the image of Jesus of Nazareth, our brother and our Lord. Catherine LaCugna's summary words are lyrical: "Jesus is what God is: infinite capacity for communion. Jesus is what our own humanity was created to be: theonomous, catholic, and in communion, in right relationship, with every creature and with God. He is who and what God is; he is who and what we are to become. Jesus owes his whole existence, authority, identity, and purpose to God; he 'originates' from God, is begotten of God, and belongs eternally to the life and existence of God. Through him we, too, originate from God, are begotten of God, and belong eternally to the life and existence of God."[12]

Paul writes that the whole "creation waits with eager longing for the revealing of the children of God" (Rom 8:19). The love of Father for Son, and Son for Father is confirmed in the love of the Holy Spirit who is generated from the Father's love in its reception in the Son. We also are given to see, appreciate, and appropriate the love of the Father of all mercies and of Jesus equal in all compassion, because we are given the Holy Spirit, who is the love of God poured out in our hearts to illumine our minds and enkindle our hearts. Thus God begets both the gift and its reception in us. God would not have us miss the incalculable treasure of the God who comes to us as God who loves in God. The Holy Spirit is "as the One who builds the Kingdom of God within the course of history and prepares its full manifestation in Jesus Christ, stirring people's hearts and quickening in our world the seeds of the full salvation which will come at the end of time."[13]

Gloria Patri: An Exchange of Love

In his autobiography, Lawrence of Arabia reports meeting an old man in the desert who said to him only these pregnant words: "the love is from God and of God and towards God."[14] In terms of our discussion of "as it was in the beginning, is now, and will be forever" one might see a parallel. The love is from the *beginning*, of *now*, and *will be forever world without end.* Accordingly we are to live from God, with God, and for God in others. The pristine glory *as it was in the beginning* is from God. The hidden glory *as it is now* is of God. The revealed glory *as it will be forever* is towards God. The text quoted could easily be shaped to a reflection on the Trinity—the love is from the Father, of (through) the Son, and to (in) the Holy Spirit.

When we do not live from God and for others (in God), we pretend an independence that is not ours as a creature, and we do not manifest an imitation of the shared life of the Trinity of divine persons. We are interdependent creatures, neither self-sufficient nor unendowed with our own personal destiny. And in this way we mirror to some shadowy extent the life of the Trinity, in which each person is fully for the other and yet who they are and no one else. Each divine person is unique and altogether given over to the other. God is alone (all one) and all together. Mutual life is Trinitarian life, and while we will never comprehend the mystery of God, we can draw implications for our own life in the image of the one God in three persons. When we pray the lesser doxology, these many implications might echo in our minds and hearts—even if not all of them and not always—because these prayer words remain inexhaustible.

On the one hand, when human relations lapse into dependency, we find that we are receiving and not giving. While it is blessed to receive, and "what do you have that you did not receive" (1 Cor 4:7), dependence sets up a relationship of indebtedness and not a friendship of equality and mutuality. On the other hand, when human relations lapse into independency, we find that we are giving and not receiving. While it is blessed to give, and "God loves a cheerful giver" (2 Cor 9:7), independence sets up a relationship of impoverishment for a creature whose resources are limited and who is never self-sufficient. Even God who is uniquely self-sufficient lives in the tri-unity of persons in a full giving that is a full receiving, and a full receiving that is a full giving. "The idea of a Person out of whose womb the Son is begotten, the fecund, ecstatic God who is matrix of all, moves us away from the idea of person as self-sufficient, self-possessing individual, which is perhaps the ultimate male fantasy."[15] In God it remains blessed both to give and to receive, and never in the life of God within the persons of God is there the one without the other.

When we acknowledge the symbiosis of a life in which giving is receiving and receiving is giving, we can understand how the praise of God in the passage of our lives unfolds in daily worship. God's gift becomes our gift of life. Our return of God's gift in the living of our life "through him, with him, and in him" becomes our gift in God's gift to us. And in the ending as in the beginning "God may be all in all" (1 Cor 15:28). Our prayerful liturgy is not inserted in our world, but breaks out in the thanksgiving of our hearts. As Aidan Kavanagh puts this truth: liturgy is not about God, liturgy is of God.[16] Living faith is faith in the communion of Father, Son, and Holy Spirit, and we speak and live out what we in truth are—"I in them and you in me, that they may become completely one, so that the world may know that you have sent me and have loved them even as you have loved me" (Jn 17:23). In sum, the Trinity is "the summary of Christian faith, not its premise."[17] And in the ending as in the beginning "God may be all in all."

Let us ask yet a further question. What then is unique about the Trinity? We might say we now know that theological "person" is more constitutive of *being* than philosophical "substance." God is infinite consciousness. God is relationship of persons. God is community and communion. God is never all alone, never the model of independence uninvolved at heart. God in Trinitarian life is ever giving all and ever receiving all in a self-imparting and self-communicating that is boundless joy. God is essentially relational. Consider that "the whole Being of God belongs to each of them as it belongs to all of them, and belongs to all of them as it belongs to each of them."[18] The Father may be imagined by us as "I" in relation to the Son ('Thou"), who in mutual love of the Spirit is "We." In God personal intimacy is the divine life.

Because with the "persons" of God "to be" is "to be for," we might well conclude that human personhood is also giving and receiving. Human society should be considered a way to live from and for others. "To be a person is to be constitutionally ec-static (or exocentric); persons come into being by their relation-ship with others."[19] Accordingly, social justice might be seen as constitutive of Church, and not just an activity. The option for the poor might not be optional, because the essence of personhood in-sists that the only way to be oneself is to give oneself away to oth-ers. "To talk about a subject or person is to talk about intersub-jectivity. Desire, which is the shaping and driving force of the person, is fulfilled only in intimacy. Thus human beings, being in desire, in-exist one another, or they remain less than human, unfulfilled in essence. This is the universal fact about human beings. . . . They actualize that mutual inexistence which is the essence of personhood."[20]

Only with difficulty do we discover who we are as we un-cover God's unique love for us. Our gift of self when we love an-other is our gift of self-identity—who we are. Of course we also give what we are, but what we are varies and what we are can be shared in many ways with other people. But when we give not only what we are but also who we are, we give a unique gift. We are no one else, and no one else can give our self away. Unlike God, whose Word is God's son, we need many words to say who we are and to give our self in ways that truly bestow us.

Let us focus again on the life of the Trinity and how it might impact the praying of the lesser doxology. Imagine that you could give yourself not over time but all at once and in an instant. Imag-ine that you could condense all your words, millions of them, into one word. Imagine all the stars and planets now flying apart at the speed of light were collapsed into each other with such concentra-tion that the entire cosmos was contained in one speck of super-dense matter so potent that its explosion would fill the void for millions of light years of expanding, interstellar space. Imagine the infinite God of love giving God's loving self in one Word, so essential and so perfectly expressive that the gift of who the Father is generates the Son as the perfect image of the Father, equal in all being to the Father, but now in love with the Father and the Father with the Son, two divine persons, yet only one infinite God outside of whom there is nothing. God spoke God's unique Word and God birthed the Word of God, of one substance with the Father, in whom love beyond telling would flow back and forth from all eternity—God in love with God ever enfolded. Imagine then the Word of God, the one unique Word of God, who is the Son of God eternally begotten in love of the Father and reciprocal love for the Father, an infinite mutuality without beginning and without ending. Try to comprehend the ineffable mystery of God who is love itself, boundless love, love spoken in a Word silent yet more potent than any explosion of a universe of a billion galaxies. In such a God, love is more bright than the stars, love more expansive than all the light years of space and time in this world. No wonder Dante ends his "Divine Comedy" with the consummate line about "the love that moves the sun and the other stars."

God's love can have no object outside of God's infinite being—which God *is*, not being that God has. In God, subject and object are identical. There is nothing outside of the infinity of God to attract God. God is everything. God is love—infinite love. Yet God's love spills over in endless cascades of love. The love of the Father for the Son remains an endless reciprocation. "Their being with and toward and for one another is identical with their being themselves; they are one with one another as ultimately as they are one in themselves."[21] And creation itself is patterned in some way on the Father's love for the Son, which cannot be contained. God implodes in the love of Father for the Son, and the Son for the Father, and both loved in the Holy Spirit. God explodes in the world created outside of God, a world remaining mysteriously inside the God who is everything. How could anything escape everything? The love of Jesus for his Father (and for us) coalesces in the mystery of the love of the Father of mercies for absolutely everyone and everything.

Gloria Patri: The Heart's Desire

As the proverb says, tell me who your friends are and I will tell you who you are. Our identity is comprised of our relationships. We are God's children, and, in addition, we are the son or daughter of, the brother and sister of, the wife or husband of, the friend of, and so forth. Relationships make human beings who we are. But we *have* relationships. God *is* relationship. We have being. God is being. We have others. God is "others"—Father, Son, and Holy Spirit—three Persons in one God. "Love most ultimately has to do with mutual joy in a mutual possession of the same treasure of being by persons who are totally aware of their otherness as distinct persons and their being with and for one another."[22] Only God loves in that vein and to infinite perfection.

Human love affairs are rarely altogether happy affairs. How can I be devoted to the one I love and still keep my own life? How else would I have anything to give? And yet I want to give myself and I need to give myself. If we only give of ourselves, however, we run the risk of smothering another with our love. They may become indebted and unable to respond. And we want them also to give, and to give as much as they receive. The balancing act that is undertaken seems awesome, and even with a net of tolerance and forgiveness we carry around the bruises of a wire-walk that can be very trying.

The same dilemma appears in our human love for God. We yearn for someone whose very thought and very being is all for us. Only God fills that desire. We want union with the God who made us and whose loving thought of us still contains us and sustains us in our very existence. And yet we want to be ourselves, other than God, yet bonded with the God who loves us and knows us from the inside out and from head to toe. We want the relationship we have to be the relationship that we are in the mystery of our existence.

Only God knows what it is to be altogether for the other— the Father for the Son and the Son for the Father—and as well to be unique and fully oneself. The Father is not the Son and the Son is not the Father. Yet both are of one being (substance), share everything totally and equally, give everything to another and still remain themselves—so much so that the Father, Son, and Holy Spirit remain one God, infinite and undivided. "In the Trinity no person wants to keep anything for themselves and in this too the Trinity is the model of friendship."[23] We wish we could love others like that, giving all and yet remaining who we are, receiving another completely yet staying the same person, giving and receiving in reciprocal joy. We are indeed made in the image of God, and the life of God is a life of love between the persons of the Trinity. The Father generates the Son in a unique generation that is from all eternity and implies no inequality or inferior derivation. The mutual love of Father and Son generates the Holy Spirit— one love in three persons. "The doctrine of the Trinity is a challenge to the modern cult of the individual; it teaches us to think in terms of complex webs of mutuality and participation."[24] The life of God is love. The life of love is God.[25]

Love remains a mystery to the human heart. What we know is that we are love-destined and that our yearnings are everyone's yearnings. We can make a powerful argument for the Trinity, as we know of God's life in the gospels, as a model of personal friendship for human beings. We are to love each other as the divine persons love one another. Our love, of course, will not be God's love in essence, but a human love assisted by grace to be a love as Jesus loved us in the love of the Father and the Son: "I in them and you in me, that they may become completely one, so that the world may know that you have sent me and have loved them even as you have loved me" (Jn 17:23). "The Trinity is the model of friendship because it is the model of oneness between persons, and it is by persons being one in and with the Trinity in knowledge, glory, and love, and telling one another about it that they are friends as Jesus wills them to be and gives them power to be."[26]

The Trinity is a model for human community because the Trinity is a model of non-exclusivity. None of the persons in the mystery of God keeps anything to themselves. Every bit of divine life is shared equally, while yet each person keeps identity and is not merged into a facile unity. "Unity of distinct persons is thereby revealed to be the most perfect kind of oneness and relations between distinct persons is revealed to be as ultimate as being itself. Because the Trinity is the model of friendship, the distinction of human persons and oneness between them is also revealed as an ultimate value, whatever the differences because God is God and we are not."[27] In God, all humanity can be comprehended as one humanity despite our differences. "As it is, there are many members, yet one body" (1 Cor 12:20). We are the people of God the Father, the body of Christ, the temple of the Holy Spirit. We are the Church, the icon of the Trinity in mutual giving and receiving, without separation or subordination. "Living from others and for others is the path of glory in which we and God exist together."[28]

If matters stand as described, if we in our human friendship reflect the mystery of the Trinity, we have cause to celebrate. The persons of the Trinity "eternally celebrate one another's being with infinitely exalted knowledge of and love for one another."[29] Therefore, let us celebrate one another created in the image of God, the image of the Trinity. "For there to be true friendship, the mutual choice and decision must be to make an irrevocable pledge of eternal fidelity to affirming and celebrating one another's being and of making existence a joint project."[30] If Christians know their dignity and their destiny together, they will live according to their eternal and cosmic being before God. We stand as immortal persons before God, persons invited into the very inner life of knowing and loving eternally that is the Trinity of God. Such love reveals what most makes human beings human. "The saints are those who have been converted by the gospel, who live in conformity with the truth of their own personhood, whose exercise of sexuality is a blessing, who are detached from wealth, whose words build up not denigrate others, who devote themselves to the service of others."[31]

Gloria Patri: The Name of God

All human beings have a secret name. Our parents give us our public name at our birthing. God, who is our creator and both father and mother to us in our very existence, also gives us a name, one that is unique and hidden from the world and known only to God. God names us, and we are God's beloved forever. God also has a secret name, but because God always was from all eternity and never was birthed into existence, no one gave God a name. God's secret name and God's mysterious being are one and the same. Jesus, the only human being who knew the Father—"the Father and I are one" (Jn 10:30) and "whoever has seen me has seen the Father" (Jn 14:9)—calls upon God as *Abba*. Therefore *Abba* (Father) could be construed as the hidden name of God, in so far as human language can comprehend infinite divinity. Just as Jesus is God with us in human nature, so the name *Abba* is God with us in human language. Hence the wording of the doxology, "glory to the *Father* and to the *Son*" might enjoy a special pleading.

Because there remains a feeling among many women in the Church that in practice "if God is male, the male is God,"[32] the language of the doxology has not been without objection. If patriarchy gains support from masculine imagery and noninclusive language in prayers, hymns, or scriptures, surely something should be done to lessen the complaint that God is unfairly masculine in our liturgy. "Glory be to the creator, the redeemer, and the sanctifier" has been suggested as an alternative wording for the doxology.[33] We do attribute creation of the world to the Father, redemption on the cross to the Son, and the holiness of the Church to the Holy Spirit. At the same time, we know the Father, Son, and Spirit are one God, and all the outreach of the Holy Trinity in this contingent world is the action of all three persons in the one infinite God. Might we argue that Father should be understood not as arbitrary metaphor but as the proper name of God, the *Abba* God, the otherwise unknown personal name of God revealed to us by the one who said "not that anyone has seen the Father except the one who is from God; he has seen the Father" (Jn 6:46)? Might we claim that creator, redeemer, and sanctifier could be construed as substituted proper nouns referring to the unknown mystery of God? In speculation one might do so, but there is less support in the prayer tradition of the Church. "Glory be to the Creator" has little biblical warrant comparable to the "Glory be to the Father." For that reason, and because creator, redeemer, and sanctifier are likely to be misunderstood as particular activities attributed misleadingly to only one divine person of the Trinity, such a proposed change to the doxology, even well intentioned and received with sympathy, is not likely to prevail in Church prayer.

If fatherhood is a virtue of God, just as love, goodness, and justice are qualities of God, then motherhood belongs to God just as well. One might argue that God is both father and mother, and neither father nor mother, as we understand those human characteristics. God is not made in our image. We are created in God's image, and human fatherhood/motherhood are a reflection of God's parenting, not the other way round. Nonetheless, it is true to say that God is equally fatherly and motherly, even if we do not comprehend what those qualities known to us from human experience would be in essence in the very divine being of God.

Although the Bible shows a predominance of masculine images and metaphors to describe God, the maternal is not absent. Isaiah has the Lord God say: "can a woman forget her nursing child, or show no compassion for the child of her womb? Even these may forget, yet I will not forget you. See, I have inscribed you on the palms of my hands" (Is 49:15–16). And Jesus in the gospel weeps over the holy city: "Jerusalem, Jerusalem. . . . How often have I desired to gather your children together as a hen gathers her brood under her wings, and you were not willing! (Mt 23:37). And other examples abound. Whether or not such argument is enough to explain the origins of the masculine in the language of God and to give justification to the traditional linguistic ways of both biblical and liturgical usage, surely we can agree that to the extent that the feminine in the biblical language of God has been overlooked it should be noticed and fully incorporated in the liturgy. That result would not be so much to subtract from the name of God as Father, but to make a fair space for the use of an appellation of God as Mother. Obviously the gender of Jesus is masculine, although equally compelling is the recognition that what is crucial about the incarnation is not the gender of Jesus but the humanity. *Et homo factus est* is by no means the equivalent of *Et vir factus est,* even though this infelicity of the English language cannot distinguish between man (male gender, *vir*) and man (human being, *homo*).

Jesus called God, "*Abba,* Father" (Mk 14:36), and given the intimacy of Jesus with *Abba,* his Father, one concludes that Jesus is using *Abba* not as a name for God from among many in a stable of human metaphors, but rather that "Father" stands as an unique name for God, a hidden and mysterious name of God, the name of God revealed by Jesus, the name of God not revealed to Moses at the burning bush in the desert when the Lord God answered Moses' question "who are you" with those words of mystery and silence: "I am who I am" (Ex 3:14). The trouble with privileging Father in Christian prayer does not stem from reading Father as the proper name of God revealed only to Jesus and then to his disciples. Jesus said of our customary use of Father, "And call no one your father on earth, for you have one Father—the one in heaven" (Mt 23:9). Uppercase Father is never to be confused with lowercase father, whose meaning is derived from human experience. The trouble with our use of Father in prayer is that we tend to hear it only as a human metaphor to describe a quality in God based on masculine virtue and biology in this world. We need to be more sensitive to how the word is intended. One's God remains too small, one might object. The Father is more than human words can say, and the name points to the divine being whose name is ineffable. *Abba* should not be presumed just as YHWH was not voiced. We would not presume to say the secret name of God unless Jesus had told us that when we pray that we might dare to say "Our Father."

Let us conclude our reflection on the Trinitarian wording of this ancient prayer. The lesser doxology is but a few chosen words. The first part of that prayer names the persons of the Trinity and acknowledges simply the glory that is God. The second part of the doxology speaks of that glory in time past, time present, and time future. But there remains only one Trinity in this prayer of two parts. Eternity encompasses time. God in God's self (immanent theology of the Trinity) and God for us (the economy of the Trinity in human history) form only one exclamation of worship. Catherine LaCugna writes so well of these matters:

> God goes forth from God, God creates the world, God suffuses its history and dwells within us, redeeming the world from within. God makes an eternal gift to the world of God's very self. Through the outpouring of God into our hearts as love, we become by grace what God is already by nature, namely, self-donating love for the other.
>
> In both the eternal and temporal existence of God, it is the nature of God to-be-for, to-be-toward, to exist as persons in communion. God initiates and sustains intimate, covenanted relationship with a people, God takes on flesh and undergoes death, God dwells in our hearts, because God lives from all eternity as self-communicating, self-giving love and communion. God incorporates all of creation into that life of communion. It is in this sense that we literally exist, we 'have our being' in God. *The life of God does not belong to God alone.*[34]

"As It Was in the Beginning"—
The Glory of Eternity and Time

In the beginning speaks of both eternity and time. In the beginning could mean always in all eternity, which has no beginning in time. In the psalms we read: "Lord, you have been our dwelling place in all generations. Before the mountains were brought forth, or ever you had formed the earth and the world, from everlasting to everlasting you are God" (Ps 90:1–2). In the epistles of Paul we read: "But we speak God's wisdom, secret and hidden, which God decreed before the ages for our glory" (1 Cor 2:7). In the gospel we read: "In the beginning was the Word, and the Word was with God, and the Word was God. He was in the beginning with God. All things came into being through him, and without him not one thing came into being" (Jn 1:1–3). Augustine writes: "You [O God] created all times and you exist before all times" and "Time could not elapse before you [O God] made time."[35] *In the beginning* could also mean as it was from the first day, from the beginning of time itself, "In the beginning when God created the heavens and the earth" (Gen 1:1). We need binocular vision to read this text with the fullness of eternity and the fullness of time that it deserves.

To reflect more on the relationship of time and eternity, let us explore the prior mystery of creation itself. How can there even be a creation? If God is infinite, if God is everything, how can something be anything? That is the mystery of the One and the Many, and a master key to philosophy and to theology. How can there be a creation if the creator is infinite? Given everything, there is no room for something more. How can the world exist apart from God? And if the world is but God made manifest, then we are not creatures somehow outside of God and capable of true relationship with God. At the same time, and nonetheless, if God is all being, then creation cannot be outside of God. Paradoxically, created beings exist truly outside of God and yet truly inside of God as well ("outside" and "inside" understood as inadequate metaphor). Given one and only God, who by the divine nature must be infinite in order to be the only God, then creation itself is a profound mystery.

The mystery of the One and the Many might be seen as a corollary to the mystery of the Trinity, one God in three divine persons. Each person of the Trinity gives everything and receives everything of divinity. Each gives all and each receives all. The Many of creation is also fully given by God as a creation outside of God, and the One is fully received by a creation that can never in all its immensity be outside of God who is infinite everything. The mystery of creation remains somehow truly something made out of nothing. God alone can give it away and yet keep it. God alone can be all poured out and yet all contained and everlasting fullness. When God withdraws, God creates. Yet God is never away, but now and here always and everywhere. God is the One of infinity, and God encompasses the Many of a finite world. This mystery of God who is everything, and yet created everything of this world as a world apart from God yet not separated from God, gives rise to any number of paradoxes. This God of mystery is infinite largesse and boundless being, both distant and near, transcendent beyond this world and immanent within its smallest speck, and more part of me that I am part of myself.

If God is everything, even though the creation is something that is not God and yet cannot be outside of everything that is God, wonders never cease. For example, God is not one more person in the room, but bigger than the rest of us. God is not one more cause in the universe, but more potent than the physical causes we measure. God is above and below us, around us everywhere and nowhere. God is altogether in us; better yet, let us say we are all together in God who surrounds us and permeates all that exists. God is not in history as one more actor and the most powerful; all of history is in God. And yet we are not God, nor any part of God, nor ever apart from God. "In him we live and move and have our being" (Acts 17:28). How such a mystery of God can be is not knowable to us in this world. Only when we are given to see God face to face will we know God, the *mysterium tremendum,* in such depth unto the capacity of our creaturehood elevated by divine grace.

One might think we have come a far way from doxology, but not so. God's glory is also our glory by participation, and the glory we give to God is God's glory from the beginning. Consider the Byzantine liturgical formula: "we offer Thee Thine own, of what is Thine own, in all and for the sake of all." The One and the Many can be transferred to the one glory and the many glories of doxology. "The uncertainty as to whether the opening phrase of the *Gloria* refers to the glory which God receives from human worshippers or angels, or to that which He possesses and which radiates from Him, is itself crucial to His identification, for there is nothing which can be offered to God which is not already continuous with His being. . . . [T]he ambiguous lineaments of glory underline the theological nature of donation, for although we offer the gifts of praise, blessing, adoration, and glory to God, He is not a discrete donée who merely 'receives,' but radiates outwards in glory which overtakes and makes possible our offerings even before they are offered."[36]

The One and the Many: Creation and Providence

Why anything? That question has fascinated philosophical minds from ancient times. If one believes in God the creator, that question becomes only the more profound. Where does one's existence come from? Where does one's life come from? The procreation of human life, of course, stems from the human family. My mother and father gave me my life. They created for me my body from their bodies. And yet I want to say it is even more true that God created me. God has created all things and all people, though our created forebears stand as pro-creators within God's creative amplitude. We are within God's mystery, yet nowise pantheistically are we part of God. How creation from nothing is even possible remains within the profound mystery that is God.

Let us deepen the mystery of God yet more. Not only is God implicate in all existence, God is sovereign over all activity in the world. Whatever happens in the world is all God's doing and at the same time all the doing of the world. The providence of God is a corollary of the infinity of God, and the providence of God in the realm of doing is the dynamic parallel to the creation of God in the realm of being. Providence is the mystery of the One and the Many in the realm of dynamics. Such is the fullness of the glory of God.

When we lose some object in our daily round, we may have been taught to pray to St. Anthony of Padua to find what is lost. And I have found it works, most of the time. If you want a natural explanation, I can give you one. When we pray with hope of a response from heaven, we become more peaceful and less agitated about our loss. That reduction in stress facilitates the unconscious mind to prompt us about where we left the lost article.

If you want a providential explanation, I can give you one as well. God's providence does everything, creates and sustains everything, prompts us to pray and to search. There is nothing that happens that is not fully God's doing even while our own accomplishment. We can and probably should pray for our next breath, and I have found myself praying for the rising of the sun. Can I not take my next breath? Does not the sun rise inevitably by the immutable laws of physics? Well, yes and no. Yes, I can breathe on my own and the sun will rise, and no I cannot breathe nor will the sun rise without God's sustaining providence. Is then everything God's doing? Is then God in everything done? I prefer to claim that everything done is in God. God is not one more actor. Better said, all activity remains within God's providence. God is not one more cause in the world. All causes are within God. God is everything; God is doing everything. And yet we are created apart from God who is everything, and we freely act even though God is doing everything. *Mysterium tremendum.* Glory . . . as it was in the beginning, is now, and will be forever.

Let us explore once again the wonder of the God to whom we give all glory. All being gives glory to God whether it knows it or not, chooses it or not. The glory of God is revealed not only in the infinite being of God who is mysteriously implicated in all things, while at the same time creating a world outside of God and yet somehow inside God. The glory of God is also manifest in the infinite doing of God as well as in the being of God. Whatever happens is God's activity. God is not just watching everything. God is doing everything, and yet the activity of physical nature, of human freedom, and of random chance are genuine causes (just as we are real created beings) somehow outside of God's doing everything and yet altogether inside God's sovereign providence. I believe God is the Lord of all doing, even the Lord of chance. How God provides for us all while not contaminating the integrity of this world's causes remains the very mystery of God. God is doing everything, but so are chance, human freedom, and the laws of physics doing everything. That is the glory of God, who remains everything and creates a world of something, who does everything and enables human freedom for anything.

We can have some vague understanding of how events might be designed and yet be spontaneous. The casino owner does not know how every chance spin of the wheel will turn out, but the owner knows the house will make a profit. The husband or wife who times a suggestion with an eye to the characteristic responses of their partner may obtain their way even while the other is taking all the credit and responsibility. The modern laws of physics are consistent provided the context is stable, but more contemporary quantum physics claims no predetermined outcome. My examples above do not explain the sovereignty of God, but they hint at the mystery of an infinite God who has the whole world in his hands and yet gives the world its complete integrity. Chance is real chance. Freedom is real freedom. Physics is real law. And yet God remains sovereign over all. The glory of God remains more a verb than a noun, more an ineffable mystery unknowable than a thesis for logical investigations.

We sometimes imagine that the world is an errant satellite that God launched long ago. Now the world is lost in space. No one can any longer guide its direction. It wobbles about and will crash at some unforeseen time and place. God watches like "ground control" become helpless, wringing hands on the sideline, hoping all turns out for the best. In this picture God apparently is not omnipotent. God has become impotent in the face of forces that God created. Similarly we recognize how human parents bring children into life and then watch anxiously as they in their freedom move beyond their parents' control, if they ever were within control. To the contrary, however, we believe God is not helplessly watching the world, nor is God only assisting us: God is allowing us all final determination of the outcome of creation. God is doing everything with sovereign wisdom, power, and goodness. As the song sings so disarmingly—"he's got the whole world in his hands." Neither the vast cosmos nor the little baby is beyond God's constant providence. That divine care in the midst of a world on its own way is the mystery of God and the infinite glory of God. Listen to the implications of the oration at morning prayer in the Divine Office for Monday of Week One: "Father, may everything we do begin with your inspiration and continue with your saving help. Let our work always find its origin in you and through you reach completion. We ask this through Our Lord Jesus Christ, your Son, who lives and reigns with you and the Holy Spirit, one God, for ever and ever."

The mystery of God we are speaking about suggests in God an infinite plenitude. God is nothing but resourceful. God is not outwitted nor outrun. God is the "hound of heaven" not to be thrown off the scent. God has endless ways to reach the human heart and soften its hard heartedness. Death also, one may counter, is resourceful. Death has endless ways of pursuing its prey. Death catches up with everyone at the end. Death is so resourceful that it finds a way around all the defenses of life and the living. But the Bible argues that God's love is equally strong, equally tenacious, equally resourceful. "Strong as death is love" (Sg 8:6). God's love has endless ways of courting the beloved. Love—God's love—catches up with everyone in the end. God is infinitely resourceful, more resourceful than even death. God finds a way around all the defenses of sin and the ravages of death. God is strong love, and God is sovereign in the ending as in the beginning. Such is the mystery and the glory of the providence of God—"as it was in the beginning, is now, and will be forever."

Belief and Decision

Let us explore further implications of God as *mysterium tremendum,* which I believe the Gloria Patri invites us to contemplate in the very distilled wording of such pure mystery. I never met an atheist, though I am sure there are those who do not believe in God. The self-proclaimed atheists I know are mostly confused. When asked to describe the God they deny, I feel compelled to add that if that is who or what God is, neither do I believe in God. I want to say: "You have made an idol, and you have enough sense to recognize that such a mirage is unworthy of your credence." I conclude it would be better to watch how a person lives their life than to listen to their words about God. Few people know the language to speak of the unspeakable. Thus, they do not mean what they say about God, nor do they say what they mean about God, and what they hear is not what was said. But they do confess what they believe by the way they live. I am not so much interested in moral virtue, as if a good ethical life is proof of one's belief in God, because moral virtue is often its own reward. Rather I look to hope beyond despair. Believers think life has meaning. They hold out in some way for truth, for goodness, and for beauty, which in their transcendence can come only from God. Where there is smoke there is fire. I look for those people who recognize the human condition is enveloped in smoke.

Despair suggests bone-level disbelief, though it may not be possible to know who embraces despair. One can despair of this world, or one's self, and not despair of God. Here again, in our despair we do not always say what we mean nor mean what we say. Perhaps no one knows truly who believes in God. Those who claim they believe in God should not be presumptuous, for who can read his or her own heart as it appears before God? And those who claim they do not believe in God should not despair. In their heart of hearts, in their distress, there may be hidden grace. When the prosecution asked Joan of Arc in her trial whether she knew she was in the grace of God, her adversaries thought she could not answer without condemning herself. If she said yes, she would be presumptuous, and if she said no, she would discredit the visions she was willing to die for. What she said simply in her graced wisdom we all must say: "If I am not [in grace], may God put me there; if I am, may he keep me there."[37]

So much depends on where one begins. In all our thinking we must assume a starting point, and that is a personal decision. You cannot deduce the starting point of your thinking about God, for that would presume a prior beginning and a more original source out of which further thought might flow. For example, do I stand first as a rationalist at heart and add to that identity my religious faith, or do I claim that I am at heart God's contingent creature and add to that my enlightened reasoning? One might imagine the operating system that comes installed with a new computer. Subsequent operations depend on the initial start-up. One cannot expect further operation if the basic language system is not already chosen (booted, as it is colorfully described). In our minds, what is our operational system? Where do we begin? "I am who I am; is there a God?" Or, "God is obvious and necessary, who am I?" The former stand makes me the center and calls God into question. The latter stand makes God the center and calls me into question. My existence is the true question! Why me? Why anything? Such foundational standpoint comes from a deep personal choice. Over a lifetime this profound decision evolves into a simple yes or no to our human life as a given. This commitment is so deep, however, that it may not be readily available to our human consciousness. Most of all, such choices flow from God's hidden grace in our lives. Our behavior may give a clue to where we stand before God, but it yields only a surmise. Let not those who cannot speak of God despair, and let not those who have religious rhetoric become presumptuous. God knows and only God knows. And hence let the glory be to God.

Providence that is identical with the mystery of God does not yield an understanding of evil in the world. The mystery of God grows only deeper. We human beings would probably not have made a world where soft flesh and hard earthquakes intersect. God is responsible, nevertheless, for the world God made, and both human flesh in its freedom and vulnerability and the cosmos in its physical genesis remain the very good world that God chose. God is indeed answerable for a world where accidents can happen. God is not responsible, however, for every accident as if God chose to make this accident happen. In the "last judgment" not only will we give an account of our freedom (or have our freedom revealed), but God will justify the ways of God to men (in other words, God's freedom will be revealed and justified). Because God is good, we know the world God has made is good. The devil is in the details, however, and human impatience to know all does not provide us explanation now in this world.

Evil in the form of deliberate human choice and not of accident is another matter. Here the tradition has argued that sin is a no-thing, a privation of what should be and is not, because creatures can and do fail. Granted God is responsible for everything that is and everything that is done, but God is not responsible for nothing. Sin has no substance; sin has no intelligibility; sin is absurd. The Queen in *Alice in Wonderland* insists: "the verdict first, then the evidence." She does not want the truth of the way things are; she wants what she wants. In such willfulness there is nothing to be understood. Sin is non-sense. Sin is boarding a train for New York when one wanted to go to San Francisco. In sinfulness the human heart takes its stand in darkness. The effects of sin, however and alas, may be all too real on self and others.

Time and Eternity

Let us now explore a further reading of the temporal wording of the Gloria Patri. "As it was in the beginning" does not exactly claim to tell of the past, because in the beginning there was yet no past. Indeed, in the beginning there was yet no time at all. Time was created in the beginning, and now we look back on the beginning as time past. God created time. All material creation exists in time (and space). The fullness of creation, the fullness of the Many that emerged from the infinite One, is also the fullness of time. God, however, lives in the fullness of eternity that instantiates the fullness of time. God is the infinite now, the now that is unchanging and includes the past and the future as we know time. God dwells not in time but in eternity. For God there is only now. Past, present, and future are measures of our time. God is not in time; time is within God's immensity and sovereignty. The fullness of eternity is the ineffable mystery of God. Eternity is not time elongated with endless zeros. Eternity is not our created time endlessly prolonged. Eternity is the fullness of God and God is the fullness of eternity. Time, however, remains as it was in the beginning, is now, and ever will be—the creation of God.

The lesser doxology is divided into a statement and a comparison. "Glory to the Father, the Son, and the Holy Spirit" is the statement; glory "as it was, is, and will be" provides the comparison. The statement entails the fullness of God, the fullness of the infinite, the fullness of the One who is source of all being. The comparison speaks of the fullness of time in the mystery of creation, the mystery of the Many, the mystery of a reality outside of God and yet within the infinite God whose boundlessness encompasses all creation. The glory that was "in the beginning, is now, and will be forever" gives a comparison that we should read as the fullness of time enfolded in the fullness of eternity. In short, the comparison in the doxology proclaims glory to God always in time and in eternity.

The comparison of past, present, and future I want to read as the mystery of Eternity and Time, a corollary of the mystery of the One and the Many that we spoke of above. Time belongs to the created world of the Many. Thus the "was, is, and will be" refers to our created beginnings, our moment of grace now, and the future coming of God until the ending of the world and time itself. In short, the comparison in the doxology proclaims glory to God in the fullness of time initiated by God and sharing in the glory of God, as does all of creation that claims its integrity outside of God and yet cannot escape the implicate infinity of the God who remains everything and whose eternity encompasses all of time from its beginning to its ending in the sovereignty of God's providence.

Let us try again to state the richness of the Gloria Patri in its interplay of eternity and time. Instead of using the terms eternity and time, let us borrow from classical theology the term *nunc stans* (the now that stands still, that is, the world of eternity and the plenitude of being) and *nunc fluens* (the now that flows, that is, the world of time and becoming). God's immensity comprehends the infinite *nunc stans.* The created world's diversity is in the finite *nunc fluens.* Accordingly we could read the doxology comparison of "as it was, is, and will be" as a shorthand for now as glory always was and always will be, that is, now and forever (as in the beginning), the *nunc stans* of God who has no beginning and no ending. One might also with justification read the doxology comparison as an inclusion of the *nunc fluens,* which proclaims glory to God now as from the beginning of time and so forever until the ending of time. In truth, one need not choose between the *nunc stans* and the *nunc fluens* any more than we need choose between the One and the Many, the uncreated and the created, the infinite and the finite. God belongs both to eternity and also to time, or more accurately, time belongs in the eternity of God.

Human beings who live in time can give glory to God in prayer, words in time that speak of the tremendous mystery of God in the recognition of God's ineffable being that is mysteriously shared in this our creation. "You are worthy, our Lord and God, to receive glory and honor and power, for you created all things, and by your will they existed and were created" (Rev 4:11). Doxology always remains a plain truth.

If the comparison in the second part of the lesser doxology is read primarily as the amplification of the statement "Glory to God—Father, Son, and Holy Spirit" in all eternity alone, there is less added to the doxology by the comparison. If we read the comparison, "as it was, is, will be," however, as the dual glory of God in the fullness of time as well as in the fullness of eternity, then we read the lesser doxology more profoundly. The fullness of time is a rich concept, of course, worth lauding alongside of the fullness of eternity. We know more of that world of imminence than of the world of transcendence, and we shall speak below at length of the economy of salvation as we know it—past, present, and future. Given, however, that the fullness of eternity encompasses a whole theology of the Father, Son, and Holy Spirit and the very mystery of God's being, the fullness of time will encompass a whole theology of what was in the beginning, is now, and will be forever—the saving goodness of God in world and human history.

Because time and eternity co-penetrate in the moment of grace, we need to expand our commentary to talk of both time and eternity. In the incarnation of the Son of God made man, this mystery of God and man in communion is both fulfilled and revealed all at once. Jesus was both fully human and fully divine, fully in time and fully in eternity. Hence the doxology can be read both in time and in eternity. Orientation to God through Christ in the Holy Spirit dovetails well with "as it was, is now, and will be." We are reading the text in time, and we are hardly able to talk of eternity except in terms of time, for we know only time. In the beginning and in the ending also embrace eternity, but the words are of time. Let us listen to the last book of the Christian scriptures. "I am the Alpha and Omega, says the Lord God, who is and who was and who is to come, the Almighty" (Rev 1:8). All ages belong to Christ. "Holy, holy, holy, is the Lord God almighty, who was and is and is to come!" (Rev 4:8) "As it was in the beginning, is now, and will be forever" of the lesser doxology echoes well these words as well as the conclusion of the Epistle of Jude: "Now to him who is able to keep you from falling, and to make you stand without blemish in the presence of his glory with rejoicing, to the only God our Savior through Jesus Christ our Lord, be glory, majesty, power, and authority, before all time and now and forever. Amen" (Jude 24–25).

"Is Now"—The Fullness of Time and the Hidden Glory

*I*n the preceding chapter, we spoke of "in the beginning" as a corollary of the mystery of the One and the Many, the mystery of creation as the fullness of eternity that glorifies God throughout the fullness of time. In this chapter we will speak of the "is now" as the mystery of the incarnation that fulfills in the fullness of time, the mystery of the Lord Jesus as the primordial sacrament that glorifies God throughout time. In the following chapter we will speak of "will be forever" as the mystery of the New Jerusalem, the mystery of the descent of the Holy Spirit (*epiclesis*) into our lives and our communion of saints, the liturgical moment that continuously celebrates the marriage of eternity and time in the fullness of grace.

Let us now turn to a consideration of the mystery of God in the fullness of time—what Paul calls God's "plan for the fullness of time" (Eph 1:10).[38] In the simple and direct words of John the Baptist: "The time is fulfilled, and the kingdom of God has come near; repent, and believe in the good news" (Mk 1:15). Our focus will narrow on crucial events of the life of Jesus, his birth and his death and resurrection. We shall explore the glory of "is now" particularly in terms of the mystery of incarnation (Christmas) and the mystery of the cross and resurrection (Easter). And we shall claim that these mysteries in the sacraments of the Church continue to be "now" unto the everlasting glory of God.

If the evolution of planet Earth were imagined as a calendar year, life itself would first appear in October, the existence of mammals in mid December, and human beings on the last day of the year—a secular fullness of time. In the Christian scriptures the "fullness of time" speaks of the moment of the incarnation of the Son of God. "But when the fullness of time had come, God sent his son, born of a woman, born under the law, in order to redeem those who were under the law, so that we might receive adoption as children" (Gal 4:4). In that moment the past is gathered up as prologue to the Christocentric fullness of time and the future is pledged as epilogue. Past, present, and future in God's providence and economy of salvation coalesce to become the fullness of time. We read of the coming of Jesus Christ in the First Letter of Peter: "He was destined before the foundation of the world, but was revealed at the end of the ages for your sake" (1 Pt 1:20). Eternity intersects and interpenetrates time itself. "The fullness of time has come upon us at last; God sends his Son into the world."[39] Time is now revealed to be pregnant with grace, and time passing gives birth to Christ in all time. Paul writes of Jesus: "He is the image of the invisible God, the firstborn of all creation; for in him all things in heaven and on earth were created, things visible and invisible. . . . [A]ll things have been created through him and for him" (Col 1:15–17). The liturgy expresses the insistent human yearning for God's presence in the here and now:

> In joy, we wait for your coming,
>   come, Lord Jesus

Before time began, you shared life with the Father,
>   come now and save us.
You created the world and all who live in it,
>   come to redeem the work of your hands.
You did not hesitate to become man, subject to death,
>   come to free us from the power of death.
You came to give us life to the full,
>   come and give us your unending life.
You desire all people to live in love in your kingdom,
>   come and bring together those who long to see you face
>   to face.[40]

In particular the Christmas liturgy proclaims the fullness of time and the glory that "is now." The whole Advent liturgical season is conceived as patient expectation. We await the coming of the Lord. The seven "O Antiphons" call upon *Wisdom,* the *Lord God,* the *Flower of Jesse,* the *Key of David,* the *Radiant Dawn,* the *King of kings,* and *Emmanuel.* Each antiphon concludes with the summary plea: "come!" When the time has come, when the ages have passed, the Lord is come upon the earth in the stable of Bethlehem. The Hebrew Scriptures give the promise of the future Messiah; the Christian scriptures claim his presence among us. Judgment at the end time will consummate this fullness of time. "It is finished," Jesus says on the cross as he dies (Jn 19:30). "It is finished" is what we may presume the Lord Jesus, who "will come to judge the living and the dead," will proclaim at his second coming. In sum, what God has wrought "in the beginning," God will fulfill "in the ending" in the complete fullness of time, the fullness of time already present in the coming of Jesus in the flesh, "the fullness of him who fills all in all" (Eph 1:23). Now the time has come.

In the Epiphany-day liturgy there is a mystical yoking of three gospel events: "Today the Bridegroom claims his bride, the Church, since Christ has washed her sins away in Jordan's waters; the Magi hasten with their gifts to the royal wedding; and the wedding guests rejoice, for Christ has changed water into wine, alleluia."[41] The gifting by the Magi, the baptism of Jesus at the Jordan, and the changing of the water into wine at the wedding in Cana are each epiphanies. Divinity shines out where one had expected only a baby boy, only a bath with water, only water to drink. In each of these theophanies the divine is wed to the human. The bridegroom claims his bride, the people of God. The Son of God is enfleshed in the birth of Jesus, who is recognized king of kings by the Magi; the man Jesus is revealed to be "my Son, the Beloved; with you I am well pleased" (Lk 3:22); the water of our humanity is changed into the wine of our grace-transformed life. Each of these epiphanies is also a doxology, for we see the glory of God shining in this ordinary world. Recall, as we said in the second chapter of part 1, that *epiphaneia* in Greek was a candidate for the Greek translation of the Hebrew *kabod* (glory) but was rejected in favor of *dóxa* because of the pagan context that contaminated *epiphaneia*.[42] To the shepherds of Bethlehem before the coming of the Magi, the angels sang "Glory to God in the highest heaven" (Lk 2:14); at the Jordan river "the heaven was opened, and the Holy Spirit descended upon him [Jesus] in bodily form like a dove" (Lk 3:22); in Cana of Galilee "Jesus did this, the first of his signs . . . and revealed his glory" (Jn 2:11).

At the wedding feast of Cana, Jesus tells the servants to fill the six large water jars to the brim, and then commands the steward to draw the water changed into wine and serve a plentiful draught. We think of the river of time that "just keeps rolling along." Imagine now that oceans are finally filled. The flow of time has reached a fullness. It can hold no more. The yearnings of all the ages, the desires of the human heart in a thousand times and a thousand places has been pooled to a fullness like the pressing of many grapes to fill a wine vat. The fullness of time represents all that time can prepare. In that fullness of time the waters of human history become the fullness of grace, when the heavens are opened and the almighty Word of God leaps down from above in the silence of the night and becomes flesh. "Long ago God spoke to our ancestors in many and various ways by the prophets, but in these last days he has spoken to us by a Son, whom he appointed heir of all things, through whom he also created the worlds. He is the reflection of God's glory and the exact imprint of God's very being, and he sustains all things by his powerful word" (Heb 1:1-3). The water become wine is the river of baptism become an ocean of faith. The water become wine is a sign of the fullness of time in Jesus Christ our Lord.

This awareness of the fullness of time and the glory to God that "is now" is clearly revealed in the blessing of the Easter Candle: "Christ yesterday and today, the beginning and the end, Alpha and Omega, all time belongs to him, and all the ages, to him be glory and power through every age for ever. Amen." The biblical text echoes the liturgical text: "I am the Alpha and the Omega, the first and the last, the beginning and the end" (Rev 22:13). Or, "Jesus Christ is the same yesterday and today and forever" (Heb 13:8). In the Jerusalem Bible the translation from Hebrews is even more germane: "Jesus Christ is the same today as he was yesterday and as he will be for ever." The doxological prayer we are considering surely echoes these biblical texts: "Glory . . . as it was in the beginning, is now, and will be forever, [world without end]. Amen."

Incarnate Glory

Let us explore further implications of the "fullness of time." There is a difference between a gift from oneself and a gift of oneself. The gift from oneself comes from one's largesse, however large or small. The gift does carry something of one's regard for the beneficiary on a continuum that runs from the polite social gift to the heartfelt personal gift. Nonetheless, such a gift is not a self-gift. Such a gift is not the gift of one's person, body and soul. We have no more precious gift to give than our self. "With my body I thee wed," consummates the marriage vows. With the gift of myself I thee gift. That kind of self-gift is by its nature so total and complete that one can give oneself away only "once and for all." If one can give self away more than once, something has been held back. One can have many friends, but only one spouse if one's self-gift is once and for all. With God, that difference between gift and self-gift is the difference between the creation as gift of God and the incarnation of the beloved only Son of God as the very self-gift of God, given once and for all. Jesus remains the unsurpassable gift and the irrevocable gift forever and ever. We read in the Letter to the Hebrews: "he [Christ Jesus] has made his appearance, *once and for all,* now at the end of the last age, to do away with sin by sacrificing himself" (Heb 9:26; emphasis mine). In giving us the Son, the Father has given us everything. Indeed, the incarnation may have been intended by God from the beginning of creation, and thus may not be motivated only as the redemption of sin and the restoration of a fallen world.

Kierkegaard tells a story of a king who falls in love with a humble maiden. Since the king is sovereign, he could marry a penniless maiden no matter what the court thought of his beloved. Free as the king might be in his own choice, he does not want his intended bride to be beholden to him for everything she would possess. All her life as queen she would be indebted to him for her position, her wealth, and for his initiative that brought her to such exaltation. But the king wants their love to be reciprocal. He thought to give her up, for the situation seems beyond resolution. She is poor; he is rich. She is powerless; he is almighty. In his heart he struggles for a way through his predicament. Perhaps he could disguise himself, and as a humble man he would court a humble woman. But, she would have to discover he was the king sooner or later, and she would then be forever indebted. He thought to give her up, but he could not, for he loved her dearly. She was the beloved, the unique beloved, the "once and for all" beloved. And so, in the anguish of his heart and the desperation of his mind the king determined to abdicate his throne. He would no longer be king, and now he could court his humble maiden with a mutual and equal freedom between them. Alas, he also comes to recognize his jeopardy. As a humble man he might be rejected by her. And if she were to accept him, she might resent him as a humble man, for she would have been rich and powerful, and she might have preferred to be queen. And so, Kierkegaard concludes, the love of God is an unhappy and unrequited love.[43]

In the history of human spirituality, the quest for God entailed an escape from the materiality of this world. One climbed the mountain of God and left the world behind. One went up and out to find God. But in the mystery of the incarnation of the Son of God in Jesus of Nazareth we find that God is interested in coming down the mountain and being born in the stable, where the domestic animals were housed and fed. We find Jesus in the marketplace with his people rather than withdrawn in the desert. "Let the same mind be in you that was in Christ Jesus, who, though he was in the form of God, did not regard equality with God as something to be exploited, but emptied himself, taking the form of a slave, being born in human likeness" (Phil 2:5–7).

The mystery of the incarnation is unique and in religious history quite to be distinguished from appearances of God. Theophanies of God can be repeated. If God wants to appear somewhere to someone, there is no reason why God could not do so, and at multiple times and in various places. Such apparitions are repetitive because God has not done anything irrevocable. After an apparition God is transcendent as before. The incarnation of Jesus, however, cannot be taken back, because it is a self-gift *once and for all*. The enfleshment of the Son of God cannot be repeated in another time or another place, and cannot be surpassed. The embodiment of the Word of God is irrevocable. *Per impossible,* God is changed. We know the disappointment in a football game when a stunning touchdown play is revoked because a referee's yellow flag is thrown. Our hearts sink. With the irrevocable incarnation of Jesus Christ, however, our hearts should never be cast down. God is with us in the flesh forever. God has burned any bridges to back then and committed God's self in God's Son to the bodily human condition now and forever. God is with us, still with us, ever with us into eternity. Jesus sits at the right hand of the Father forever in the resurrection of his human body and in life everlasting—an intimacy we shall share with him in the creedal promise of the "resurrection of the body and life everlasting." And all this mystery is here and *is now.*

The incarnation provokes endless wonder. How could the infinite empty itself? How could eternity enter time? How could the Word of God become flesh? How can the spiritual become material? Without a body, each angel is a species unto itself, unique in its essence. Contrastingly, each human being shares the same nature of humanity. We are different from one another because our bodies are apart. Matter provides us separation and identity. In our flesh, in our history, in time and in space, in our mortality we find our name. We can be at only one place at one time. To so limit the infinite and boundless God to the bounds of our material world was indeed a scandal in heaven, the "scandal of the particular," as Kierkegaard called it. The here and now is so ephemeral. Why the Virgin Mary, when there were so many others? How could God so empty infinite divinity to belong within her womb? How was she worthy of the God of all holiness before whose glory all the angels adored from all eternity with absolute reverence? How could the human contain the divine, when not even the best of the angelic host approached such infinity? Who could have imagined? "He came a little child who made a woman cry."[44] God-with-us is now.

Ever since the enfleshment of God, the love of a particular human being need not be in competition with the love of God. God in Jesus is within the human, or rather the human is now within God. And to love the human is to love God, for Jesus is both fully human and fully divine. And now we are in the image of Jesus, the image of God, truly the image of the human. Never, therefore, should a human being be a means to an end, never human love be a temporary means to endless love. Our body will rise to live forever. Our love for one another shares in our love for God and that encompassing love is forever. "Christians, know your dignity!"[45] God has chosen you this day; indeed now is the day the Lord has made, the day to be forever, world without end.

God's glory, one might claim, is to be God who is uncreated. To be what a creature is created to be reflects God's glory. To be creature is to glorify the creator. The rocks, the plants, the animals are all saints, who remain holy before the face of God, giving glory to God by their very being and by their very existence. They are what they are. They are what the glory of God created them to be. They themselves reflect glory back to God. "The heavens proclaim his righteousness; and all the peoples behold his glory" (Ps 97:6). Only human beings, however, can escape their God-given identity. We are free to refuse our humanity. We can hold back our created gift. We can hide the glory of God that we were created to manifest. We can say "no" to God. The temptation of Satan in the Garden of Eden manifests that temptation. To elaborate the tempter's words: "Listen, you all do not want to be human. Human is bad. You have to suffer. You have to learn everything from the bottom up. You are in a fragile world with a vulnerable body. Human is limited. Human life is half a life, caught between the earth and the heavens. Be like the Gods! Don't be human. Know good and evil like the Gods do. You won't die as threatened. You will be like Gods, immortal like Gods, beyond suffering like Gods." But then there was Jesus in the garden of Gethsemane: "'Father, if you are willing, remove this cup from me; yet, not my will but yours be done'" (Lk 22:42). Human beings may reflect God's glory in the now by being human.

"In the beginning," God created human beings in God's own image, and saw that it was good. Humanity gives glory to God. God found human being good. Indeed the text of Genesis says of human creation: "*very* good" (Gen 1:31). Moreover, God did not abandon humanity because of its sinfulness, as the story of Noah's flood suggests. In the gospels, the son of God becomes human, takes on our flesh, enters our human condition, belongs to our history, throws in his lot with our destiny, suffers our death, and brings us God's life shining through the glorious wounds of his crucifixion. God gives in Jesus not an explanation of human suffering, but a demonstration of divine solidarity. The human is transfigured by Jesus, and we have become a new creation. Henceforth the human gives glory to God as it was in the beginning, *is now,* and will be forever.

Jesus rose from the dead and appeared to his disciples. The tomb was found empty, not because God needed the molecules of the earthly body of Jesus to create the risen body of Jesus, but rather because the disciples could not have believed in the resurrection of a body that they could see moldering in the grave. But Jesus did not come back to this earthly life. He ascended from a life in time and space to the life of eternity before the face of God his Father. The ascension is the completion of the mystery of the resurrection. The incarnation, the crucifixion, the resurrection, the ascension, and the sending of the Holy Spirit make up movements of one dance that is the boundless mercy of God the Father for the human children of his creative love. Consider a parallel unfolding of the human love story. The meeting of the lovers, the courtship, the decision taken in the heart to love the beloved forever, the engagement, the marriage ceremony, the intimacy of bodily intercourse, and the birth of new life all make up distinct but not separate events. That one musical score reveals many movements, but one would be hard put to declare when the love was consummated. Think of the readings at the Easter Vigil, which touch on the creation, the exodus, the prophets, the incarnation, the resurrection, the ascension, and the coming of the Holy Spirit. The salvation mystery is but one sacred marriage, the divine and the human wed through many graced moments and destined for an eternal communion.

The ascension of Jesus also reveals the hidden glory, the glory given Father, Son, and Holy Spirit now, as in the beginning, and forever more. Jesus "was lifted up, and a cloud took him out of their sight" (Acts 1:9). One might read the text as a sign that Jesus is now absent and hidden away in a cloud of unknowing. What the text is saying, however, is quite the contrary: Jesus will be inwardly present to them just as the Lord God was present to the Israelites in a pillar of cloud by day and pillar of fire by night in the crossing of the desert on the way to the Promised Land.[46] At the close of Matthew's gospel Jesus promises: "And remember, I am with you always to the end of the age" (Mt 28:19). Jesus is now hidden in the cloud but remains always with us. The Lord God spoke to Moses from the cloud on Mt. Sinai: "Now the appearance of the glory of the LORD was like a devouring fire on the top of the mountain in the sight of the people of Israel. Moses entered the cloud, and went up the mountain" (Ex 24:17–18). A "bright cloud overshadowed" the disciples when a voice from the cloud on Mt. Tabor said: "This is my Son, the Beloved; with him I am well pleased" (Mt 17:5). In the blessing of the Easter Candle at the Easter Vigil we pray: "May the light of Christ, rising in glory dispel the darkness of our hearts and minds." We see now by faith, "in a mirror, dimly" (1 Cor 13:12), in a "cloud of unknowing," but in the company of a "great cloud of witnesses" (Heb 12:1) testifying that they have known in faith the risen Lord who gave gladness to their hearts as only the Lord Jesus could do, and whom they await in joyful hope as "'the Son of Man coming on the clouds of heaven' [Dan 7:13] with power and great glory" (Mt 24:30).

In the Easter Vigil liturgy the "Exultet" is sung, and its promise of light in the darkness amplifies our consideration of the cross and resurrection become the glory of God that "is now":

This is the night when first you saved our fathers: you freed the people of Israel from their slavery and led them dry-shod through the sea. This is the night when the pillar of fire destroyed the darkness of sin! This is the night when Christians everywhere, washed clean of sin and freed from all defilement, are restored to grace and grow together in holiness. This is the night when Jesus Christ broke the chains of death and rose triumphant from the grave. What good would life have been to us, had Christ not come as our Redeemer? Father, how wonderful your care for us! How boundless your merciful love! To ransom a slave you gave away your Son. O happy fault, O necessary sin of Adam, which gained for us so great a Redeemer! Of this night scripture says: "The night will be as clear as day: it will become my light, my joy." The power of this holy night dispels all evil, washes guilt away, restores lost innocence, brings mourners joy. Night truly blessed when heaven is wedded to earth and man is reconciled with God! Therefore, heavenly Father, in the joy of this night, receive our evening sacrifice of praise, your Church's solemn offering. Accept this Easter Candle. May it always dispel the darkness of this night! May the Morning Star, which never sets, find this flame still burning; Christ, that Morning Star, who came back from the dead, and shed his peaceful light on all mankind, your Son, who lives and reigns for ever and ever. Amen.[47]

Our risen Lord is with us still. "Through him, with him, and in him in the unity of the Holy Spirit, all glory and honor is yours, almighty Father, for ever and ever. Amen."

Sacramental Glory

The continuation of the Paschal Mystery is celebrated in the sacramental ministry of the Church. We turn now to that sacramental life of the Church and especially to the Eucharist as the Lord's Supper. As we have seen, the mystery of God is the mystery of the One and the Many. In that mystery God is present even while being absent; God is everywhere even while being nowhere. God is everything even while creation is something not God and yet not outside God. God is doing everything even while human freedom, cosmic matter, and pure chance act with their own signature integrity. The incarnation but deepens this mystery of God and of God's love. Jesus is Son of God and Jesus is son of Mary. Sacraments embody and enact this mystery of God who is present and yet absent in the ordinary and everyday exchanges of our lives. God is unsurpassable and ineffable mystery. In sacraments we become aware of the divine presence even in the absence. Our risen Lord is present to us, and in the Eucharist we especially do celebrate that presence as real, here and now, and forever.

To claim that eternity is present to each moment of time, "is now," does but place the mystery of the One and the Many into the context of the passage of time. Kierkegaard argued that the contemporary Christian suffers no disadvantage in comparison with the contemporary of Jesus when he walked this earth. We who are alive today have reasons to believe and reasons not to believe, just as the contemporaries of Jesus did. Here and now eternity breaks into time, for eternity collapses past and future into the moment of grace now. To God everything and everyone is present now. Hence we stand at the foot of the cross even now. Today and now we also encounter Jesus. Eternity breaks into our time just as eternity broke into the life of Mary of Nazareth long ago. We encounter our God in Jesus Christ now. Now is the hour of our salvation. "This is the day the Lord has made." The moment of grace is a moment of eternity in time, and it is a moment of decision within time in the face of experience that can be read as faith-affirming or faith-denying. That moment of decision comes with a different array of evidence for the contemporary of Jesus and for the contemporary of today, but nonetheless, a yes or no decision is a matter of grace and our freedom, and no essential advantage or disadvantage is enjoyed no matter when we encounter Jesus in the passage of time. Enough and more than enough will be given us. Many who walked with Jesus failed to recognize him. Many who never walked with Jesus on earth now greet him. "Blessed are those who have not seen and yet have come to believe" (Jn 20:29).

Not only does it not matter when you encounter Jesus in time, it does not matter where you encounter Jesus in space. Jesus will be there, for the risen Christ is the Lord who is everywhere all of the time. Eternity is ubiquitous, ever present in space as well as in time. As we encounter the risen Jesus now and not just then in his earthly day, so we encounter Jesus firsthand in the moment of grace. The medium may be the words of a disciple of Jesus who lived long after Jesus died, the medium may be the Church in its various ministries, but the encounter with Jesus is not second-hand. In the sacramental world of grace, every encounter with Jesus is firsthand. He it is who speaks to us; he it is who touches us to heal; he it is who forgives our sins and softens our heart. Jesus comes in person; he never sends someone else to take his place, though someone else may stand in his place and be the transparent vehicle of his real presence in our life today. "If you knew the gift of God, and who it is that is saying to you, 'Give me a drink,' you would have asked him, and he would have given you living water" (Jn 4:10). Our problem is not that we are separated from Jesus by two thousand years and many thousand miles, but that we do not recognize today the visitation of the Lord of time and space, the risen Christ, Emmanuel, God with us, and "now."

At the end of the reading in the Eucharistic liturgy, the reader until recently responded, "This is the word of God." Now we are directed to say only "The word of God." Whatever the motive for the change, it reminds me of a perennial truth. The words of God in sacred scripture are not memorials of the past. We are not studying ancient history when we read the story of Moses or a parable long ago given by Jesus. This reading of the word of God is not information (what the Bible says) but proclamation—*The Word of God!* God speaks God's word to us today. Now! Listen to the word of God alive and present in our midst. We are not examining the past. God's word is examining us in the present. We are in the real presence of God's word. Listen! Behold! Attend! *The Word of God.* What has this word to say to us? Now is the moment of grace. God's eternity breaks into time. God's presence is not just recollected. God's word is present here and "is now."

We know this sacramental reality best in the sacrament of the Eucharist. The real presence of Jesus is given us. We are not just remembering his last supper. We do not give information or mere recollection such as "This is the body of Christ, in case you did not know about or did not remember the story of long ago." We are eating the bread that he prayed over. "This is my body, which is given for you" (Lk 22:19). We are not just remembering Calvary past. We are present at the reality of God's love poured out in this wine. We are now at the foot of the cross. "In fact, everything that will happen until the end of the world will be no more than an extension and unfolding of what happened on the day when the battered body of the crucified Lord was raised by the power of the Spirit and became in turn the wellspring of the Spirit for all humanity. Christians know that there is no need to wait for another time of salvation, since, however long the world may last, they are already living in the last times."[48] We say at the moment of holy communion solely this: "The body of Christ." Encounter him now. Welcome him here. You receive the Lord. The body of Christ is really present. Eternity breaks into time.

Unconditional love, regardless of time and space, touches us today, and "is now," as ever in our yesterdays.

Jesus himself is the great sacrament.[49] Jesus himself is the eternal God present in the temporal man, the infinite One somehow captured in the incarnate Many articulated in this body and this soul in this time and this place. Jesus is the great sacrament and the Church is the consequent great sacrament, the very continuation of the body of Jesus Christ throughout the ages until the end of time. The sacraments of the Church constitute moments when the Church as the body of Christ is focused so intensely that the graced presence of Jesus is assured. The Eucharist is the sacrament of sacraments, the real presence of the risen Jesus, the sacrament for which all the other sacraments are preparation or consequence. The Eucharist remains the sacrament of the real presence of the risen Christ of eternity in the now moment of time within the here space of the Church.

Those without the tangible sacraments are not necessarily without God. God is also gracing their life always and everywhere. They may not know it. They may therefore not be ready to celebrate that graceful presence, and consequently they may not amplify its benefits by their awareness of how much is being given them and all that it means for now and forever. Imagine that God is trying to feed everyone everywhere and all the time. Many people do not recognize the hand of God, and they do not open their own hands to receive as much as they might. Let us suppose now that the Christian community gathers to call upon God to feed his people. We prepare our hearts for the gifts of God by the purification of our repentance. We sing songs and walk in procession to prepare our bodies for reception. We tell the stories of how well God fed his people in times past. We claim the promises that Jesus made that he would give his body and blood as our food whenever we do this in his memory. We say his words now proclaimed by his priest. With minds and hearts prepared we receive the bread and the wine. If now we are not fed with the bread of eternal life and the real presence of the risen Jesus in infinite glory within the Blessed Trinity now, what guarantee could the promises of the gospel and the pledge of the Eucharist that Jesus gave us ever hold? If not now in this sacramental moment, when? If not here in this liturgical celebration, where? Christ remains present to humanity before and after the celebration of the Eucharist, for grace is always and everywhere, but in the Eucharist we see the burning bush, we know the visitation of the Lord, we recognize Him in the breaking of the bread. We taste him on our lips, and now we hold him in our hearts.

Karl Rahner claims that "the liturgy of the Church is the symbolic presentation of the *liturgy of the world* rather than the liturgy *in the world.*"[50] His point is that liturgy reveals and then celebrates the working of God's grace in everyday life.[51] In contrast, liturgy has also been characterized as the breaking in of grace into a world without grace. Accordingly, only if one is present to the divine liturgy in the secular world is one present to grace. Rahner argues rather for the liturgy *of the world.* Divine grace remains present always in a graced world, "what occurs always and everywhere in the ordinary course of life,"[52] but such grace is only recognized and fully celebrated in sacrament.

God's grace is given to everyone. We have only one world, a graced world and a saved world. But the knowledge of Jesus and the gospel, and of the communion of saints that is the Church, provides an enormous advantage. One knows what is being given and is invited to prepare to receive the grace of God fully, honestly, and with heartfelt conversion. God's grace can then be well lived out with thanksgiving (Eucharist), because now it will be appreciated in its wonder and its good news. Imagine that you have gone to the dentist and you are sitting in the waiting room with a toothache, apprehensive about your treatment with the dentist. Someone touches your shoulder and says, "What's that tune?" You respond, "What tune?" Then for the first time the music that has been playing all along in the waiting room goes on for you. For the first time you hear the music and you listen to it and you name that tune. Perhaps it is a love song, but you had not been listening, so self-absorbed were you in your own pain. So it is with grace in the world. With the sacraments the music goes on for us now, and we hear the word of God now, and we recognize the love song now that fills our lives whether we attend it or not.[53]

The Eucharist links Christmas (incarnation) and Easter (cross and resurrection). Christ is present in the flesh in the beginning and in the ending. Christ's love of us to the end of time is remembered as it will be forever in the *parousia*. Eucharist is the mystery of Christ from the beginning with his birth in time to the ending with his second coming unto eternity, but the mystery is sacramental. The Eucharist is not profoundly understood as physical miracle—the bread into his body much as the Cana water into wine. The Eucharist is the new creation beyond all miracle—the presence of God in a world that is not God but now can never know the real absence of God, even in our "daily bread." Christ remains with us in real presence, hidden in the cloud of faith, yet revealed in the daily bread. Tolkien tells in his fiction of a special bread possessed by the elves in the forest.[54] *Waybread* is imagined not to take away hunger, but it gives strength to walk to the end of the day. Eucharist is our daily bread, our "journey bread," the bread that does not take away the pains of this life, but strengthens us to live the gospel and walk the way of the cross.

The Eucharist gives glory to God for what God has done in the past, is doing now, and will do forever. Liturgy tells the story of the past, lives the story of the present encounter with divinity and the real presence of Jesus in each breaking of the bread throughout the ages, and promises the hope of glory with God in the future. Glory to God (Father, Son, and Holy Spirit) is glory to God yesterday, today, and tomorrow—the memory of things past (as it was in the beginning), the moment of eternity and time intersecting in the present (as it is now), and the pledge of fulfillment yet to come in the future (as it will be forever). We give glory in our worship in the Eucharist to the prodigal Father of mercies, to the magnanimous Son who has enfleshed God in our midst, and to the life-giving Spirit who ensures God's care for us will prevail over all else. The liturgy of the Eucharist presents the mystery of Jesus Christ as sacrament. It is glory to God from start to finish, and it is now.

Wonderful and important as the Eucharistic bread on the altar remains, who is at the altar is as much the work of God's grace as what is on the altar. It is the body of Christ on the altar in the bread. And indeed we should adore his real presence. It is also the body of Christ in his people at the altar and really present to him. What is transformed at the Eucharist? Bread and wine to be sure, but we also are transformed into the body of Christ. Our bodies are the bread broken and our souls the grapes crushed into wine. Teilhard de Chardin writes: "over every living thing which is to spring up, to grow, to flower, to ripen during this day say again the words: This is my Body. And over every death-force which waits in readiness to corrode, to wither, to cut down, speak again your commanding words which express the supreme mystery of faith: This is my Blood."[55] We are the mystery of Christ living in us and we living in him. We become the broken and risen body of Christ. "Christ has died, Christ is risen, Christ will come again."

When I distribute the sacred body and the precious blood of Christ at the communion of the Eucharist, I say to each person, "The body of Christ." And silently I say to myself at times what is also true: "*You are* the body of Christ." You who receive this bread that is the real presence of Jesus, you who receive the body of Christ, you who are old and young, male and female, short and tall, plain and attractive, joyful and sad, healthy and sick, sinful and graced, you—yes you—you are the body of Christ. More vulnerable than the bread in my hands is the child of God who stands before me to receive the real presence of Jesus. We

ought be even more concerned about dropping the people in our
lives than we should be about dropping crumbs of the sacred
bread. We are temples of the Holy Spirit (1 Cor 6:19), and we could
light a sanctuary lamp to honor the divine presence in us indwelling.

What happens to the Eucharistic bread is what happens
to the people of God. We are the grains of bread. We are to be
changed into the body of Christ. The bread becomes the people
of God united in the eating with the body of the risen Christ. In
him we find communion with each other. In him we find communion with the transcendent God and the incarnate Christ.
Well may one speak of the miracle of the bread made the body
of Jesus. Even better may one speak of the miracle of sinful humanity made the communion of saints. In the miracle of the
loaves and fishes one may marvel that Jesus multiplies from a
few fish and a little bread a meal to satisfy thousands. One may
equally marvel should the assembled people have shared their
food and become generous. When we think of the account of the
loaves and fishes told so marvelously in all four gospels, we might
imagine Jesus feeding so many with so little bread. It would be a
miracle in this world, for while we can multiply loaves of bread,
we cannot do so in an instant. But imagine more. Suppose the
bread was taken up from this world to become the bread of eternal
life, and the disciples fed with this bread were brought into the
kingdom of God. Empowered by God's grace they were sent to
feed all the hungers of all the people of the world with but four
gospels and seven sacraments. One may marvel most of all that
God's grace does so much with so little, whether it be the plain
bread become the bread of life or we who become the body of
Christ. "How holy this feast in which Christ is our food; his pas-
sion is recalled; grace fills our hearts; and we receive a pledge of
the glory to come, alleluia."[56] Let me quote the liturgy itself upon
the glory of our saving God with the words of the Preface to Eucharist Prayer IV:

Father in heaven, it is right that we should give you
thanks and glory: you alone are God, living and true.
Through all eternity you live in unapproachable light.
Source of life and goodness, you have created all things,
to fill your creatures with every blessing and lead all men
to the joyful vision of your light. Countless hosts of
angels stand before you to do your will; they look upon
your splendor and praise you, night and day. United with
them, and in the name of every creature under heaven,
we too praise your glory.

In the "fullness of time," human beings by the grace of God
celebrate in liturgy the love of God poured out in our hearts. We
tell the story, we rehearse the dance of love, we claim the promise of everlasting life with the Trinity. Even now by faith we shall
dwell in them and they dwell in us. "Abide in me as I abide in
you" (Jn 15:4). What *was in the beginning* remains the lavish gift
of all that exists from the prodigal Father. What *is now* remains
the love of the Father in the mystery of the cross that is the Son's
self-gift given once and for all to us in Jesus. What *will be forever*
remains the God-given reception of the gift of Father and Son, for
the Holy Spirit would have us not discard the treasure offered us.
The Holy Spirit baptizes us from within. The Holy Spirit changes
our hearts and thus brings us salvation, which is first of all God's
love to be accepted as pure gift. The Holy Spirit will be forever
the illumining of our minds and the enkindling of our hearts, so
that the dance of love we rehearse in our liturgy may be lived out
in peace and justice in this time and this place and so culminate
in the dance of love beyond telling in the kingdom of God, which
is both now and to come.

Not only should one have a faith to die for, one ought have
a faith to live for. My students are fond of saying to one another
(usually in exasperation), "Get a life." I wish they would say such
a thing more gently, for we all are in desperate need of getting a

life. And the life we need is the life of Christ, who said, "I am the way, and the truth, and the life" (Jn 14:6). Salvation is our receiving, as God's gift, a graced life in which we are able to do what he told us to do: "I give you a new commandment, that you love one another. Just as I have loved you, you also should love one another" (Jn 13:34). How has Jesus loved us? Jesus loved us more than he loved himself. Jesus embraced the human community more than he clung to his own body and soul in this life. Jesus loved us as God loves us. "This is my body, which is given for you" (Lk 22:19); "all that is mine is yours" (Lk 15:31). Take and eat! Follow me! Surely God wants us to be one with him and to love in flesh and bones like those of Jesus himself. Spread on a cross and nailed to the wood, God sought to be human with a love for us in his very bones.

To be human fully (as Jesus was human fully) is enough to be saved, but we cannot achieve full human love without God's grace. That gift of God, however, is given to everyone on the earth whether they know it or not and whether they want it or not. Hence we are all called to the transcendent love humanity is capable of. We are called to love God, to enter into conversation and eternal friendship with God. In short, everyone is asked by grace in his or her life to embrace a higher love. We are asked not just to love our neighbor as ourselves but to love one another as Jesus our Lord and God has loved us. God loved us in Jesus with a surpassing love, a love willing to lay down life itself. "No one has greater love than they lay down one's life for one's friends" (Jn 15:13). Salvation empowers human beings to love as God loves, to love as Jesus loved, to love as grace inspires us to love. In sum, we are invited in this life to love others more than we love ourselves. That is the mystery of the cross, a love even unto death. "Having loved his own who were in the world, he [Jesus] loved them to the end" (Jn 13:1). "From the human side, any self-limitation which may appear, from outside the relationship of responsive love, to be entailed in the giving of self to God is in fact experienced, inside the relationship, as the very opposite. The gift of self to God is experienced as self-realization in the free service of a God whose glory includes human salvation. *Gloria Dei vivens homo.* To take Irenaeus' words in a dynamic, teleological sense: the flourishing of human life, the well-being of humanity, is God's glory."[57] As Augustine summarizes in an aphorism filled with paradox: "Love and do what you will." In sum, salvation might be imagined thus—to love as Jesus loves, to love the things of God, to love the people of God, to want to dance with God in the mystery of God's inner Trinitarian life. We are saved from ourselves when we love others as Jesus loved them, when we love ourselves as Jesus loved us, when we love the Father as Jesus loved his Father.

Given all this amplitude of God's saving love, what can we say? Surely words only begin to tell the glory of God, but begin we must. Glory to God. Glory to God's being. Glory to God's love. Glory to God being love. That love is the mystery of God—love that created us out of love and only to be loved and to love in return. Glory to the Father and to the Son and to the Holy Spirit— as it was in the beginning, is *now,* and will be forever.

"And Will Be Forever, World Without End" – The Fullness of Grace and the Revealed Glory

In the preceding chapters we drew a parallel between the Father, Son, Holy Spirit and "in the beginning, is now, will be forever." Accordingly we talked of creation "in the beginning" and the Father as source of all created being, albeit we remain aware that whatever is attributed to the Father belongs equally to the Son and the Holy Spirit. A consideration of the incarnation of the Son of God, the Word made flesh, seemed germane to the passage of time in the present (*anno Domino*), the glory of God that "is now" in the world. In this present chapter we will consider the Holy Spirit as the ongoing love of the Father and the Son forever poured out among us and "will be forever." Pentecost with the descent of the Holy Spirit births the Church, the mystical body of Christ, and the coming kingdom of God in a new heaven and a new earth, "world without end."[58]

Let us reflect more upon this activity of the Holy Spirit. If one thinks of the Father as the source of God's gift of creation, and the Son as the self-gift of God in the incarnation, then one might think of the Holy Spirit, especially given in the community of seekers, as the inspiration of grace that enables the human soul to appropriate these gifts of God. The Holy Spirit is the graciousness of God who gives not only everything about us as gift, who gives not only the self-gift that is unsurpassable in Jesus Christ, but who also tenderly gives us the reception of this saving gift of God lest we miss out on the meaning and fulfillment of our very existence as human beings. The indwelling of the Holy Spirit constitutes a personal and divine visitation that urges us to receive God's love and to love one another as Jesus loved us. The gift and the giver merge in our ensouled body, which is the temple of the Holy Spirit, so that we can give of ourselves as God has loved us. The gift of the Holy Spirit is the indwelling of God, not only a created grace that prompts us to be receptive, but the uncreated divine presence in our soul. Through the Spirit we become alive in Christ. "I have been crucified with Christ; and it is no longer I who live, but it is Christ who lives in me" (Gal 2:20).

Shakespeare says, "ripeness is all." Timing is everything. In friendship one can give a gift too soon and one can give too late. The gift will be rejected if given too soon, when the recipient is unprepared, and the gift will be resented if received too late to appropriate its significance. Hence the gift of God's creation to us is fraught with jeopardy. We can unwittingly abuse the gift, not recognizing how much we are given. Imagine a little child given an expensive camera, and the child leaves the camera outside in the rain where it is ruined. The child may come to lament that they were given so much when they were not ready to receive. They missed the gift because the timing was premature. Hence creation itself, and most of all the self-gift of God in Jesus, can be a burden to us if it remains a gift that we recognize too late. Hence the Holy Spirit is given us as the gracious reception of God's gift. In sum, God gives the gift of creation, the self-gift of his Son, and the promised reception of the gift through the Holy Spirit, who remains not just the gift of God but also the presence of God in us, lest we miss our eternal treasure.

The Holy Spirit reveals the ongoing love of God given to this world. God so loved the world he gave his only Son (Jn 3:16). And when Jesus rose to sit at the right hand of the Father, we were sent the Holy Spirit to be our consoler, our inspiration, our spiritual life, our vivification and sanctification, the active presence of Jesus in all times and places, the love of God as the soul both of the world and of the Church—our indwelling Spirit and the breath of eternal life. In his superb sonnet, "God's Grandeur," Gerard Manley Hopkins writes of the cosmic role of the Holy Spirit as a mother dove who broods over the world of dark time until the earth breaks out of its shell into abundant and everlasting life:

> The world is charged with the grandeur of God.
>   It will flame out, like shining from shook foil;
>   It gathers to a greatness, like the ooze of oil
> Crushed. Why do men then now not reck his rod?
> Generations have trod, have trod, have trod;
>   And all is seared with trade; bleared, smeared with toil;
>   And wears man's smudge and shares man's smell: the soil
> Is bare now, nor can foot feel, being shod.
>
> And for all this, nature is never spent;
>   There lives the dearest freshness deep down things;
> And though the last lights off the black West went
>   Oh, morning, at the brown brink eastward, springs—
> Because the Holy Ghost over the bent
>   World broods with warm breast and with ah! bright
>   wings.[59]

Eschatological Implications

"Is now" may still be reckoned to be the sixth day of creation. God is still creating human beings, who seek to be human like Jesus. In the book of Genesis, God creates the world in a week of days, and on the seventh day God rests. It was the Sabbath, the day of the Lord. For Christians, Sunday was a further reach into the heart of God beyond the Sabbath rest of the Jewish faith. In the Christian faith an eighth and everlasting day rose to life. Sunday became the eighth day of creation, a day without end, neither evening nor morning, the age to come. "We move from the 'Sabbath' to the 'first day after the Sabbath,' . . . the *dies Domini* becomes the *dies Christi.*"[60] In sum, "Sunday is the proclamation that time, in which he who is the risen Lord of history makes his home, is not the grave of our illusions but the cradle of an ever new future, an opportunity given to us to turn the fleeting moments of this life into seeds of eternity. . . . From Sunday to Sunday, enlightened by Christ, she [the Church] goes forward toward the unending Sunday of the heavenly Jerusalem, which 'has no need of the sun or moon to shine upon it, for the glory of God is its light and its lamp is the Lamb' (Rev 21:23)."[61] Basil the Great writes of the eighth day in a similar vein: "This day foreshadows the state which is to follow the present age: a day without sunset, nightfall, or successor, an age which does not grow old or come to an end."[62] The end of time thus becomes the eighth day of creation, "the day the Lord has made," the day that remains forever, "and ever shall be, world without end."

Not everything is wrong about the graying of old age. We live to reach our journey's end. We want not endlessly to be becoming who we are meant to be in our deepest graced self. We want to be securely who we are and preserve what we have become by the grace of God. We want not only to pursue the good, the true, and the beautiful. We want to possess them. We want to enjoy the pursuit of happiness and not just the happiness of pursuit. The "world without end" in the doxology is secure in its celebration of an infinite love of all that is and all that can be. Our hearts are thus invited to cling to God with a bond that will not fail. We know where our treasure lies, "where neither rust nor moth consumes" (Mt 6:20). We know where our heart's desire has found its home. We want the God whose love for us does not change, and we want our love for God to be cast once and for all as an eternal and irrevocable marriage, consummating all the love we have valued throughout our changing lifetime. So we say "Glory . . . as it ever shall be, world without end." Our salvation is now at hand. Come on earth, Jesus died to rise from the dead to die no more. The world has been saved now and drawn into eternity with the risen Christ now, and yet the fullness of our salvation in the communion of all the saints is yet to come. Jesus is to come again in the eschaton at the end of time. In faith we are united to God even now as we will be in heaven, but then face to face. The glory of salvation in Christ Jesus is now and then, is now and ever shall be, world without end.

Eschatology is a Greek word that speaks of the four last things — death, judgment, and union with God (heaven) or separation from God (hell). We are born to die. Our birth was a "death" to life in the womb, just as our death in the womb of this earthly life is our birth into eternal life. One might argue that judgment is always now. We are what we are now, God knows. Judgment is not something added to us by a judge whose comprehension and compassion we await. Judgment will be the revelation to ourselves of what we have already become and who we are now, how we love, and whether we desire the dance of love that God invites us to enjoy. And yet in this life God is not done with our salvation. We have not become all that we can be. Eternity is now and yet to come, world without end.

My best insight into the mystery of how the kingdom of God is present now fully in faith, and yet we do not experience the fullness of the kingdom that will never end, stems from a metaphor taken from the state lottery. Suppose you do win the lottery. Now you have the winning ticket in your hand. You are no longer poor; you are in fact rich. And yet, you do not have a nickel in your pocket and long may it be before you do. So you are rich, but not yet tangibly rich. Eschatology is like that. We have union with God in grace now, and yet there is more to come. Eternity is now, and yet to come.

We tend to think wrongly of eternity as an eternal future or as the present extended in time without limit. But we should understand eternity and time as one more corollary of that mystery of God that we have called the One and the Many. God is all being that exists, and yet the creation is not God. Eternity is all one now, even though there exist many moments of time. In eternity everything happens in God altogether without time past or time future. God is the still point, the unmoving center around which the wheel of time revolves. God is the infinite silence, the one fullness that we delimit and break into many sounds with the noise of our created lives. God is pure simplicity that perfectly compresses all wisdom into the single ineffable Word that is infinite truth—the one Word containing and surpassing all compositions that are the created many words of our many minds. We are in time, in the *now that passes* even as I write it down. God is in eternity, the *now that perdures* and holds all being together all at once—the *mysterium tremendum*.

God-created time will have an ending as time had a beginning. The glory of God will be in the ending as it was in the beginning. Creation does not fall back into nothing but comes forward into everything. The Many that was created by the One will be implicated in the one God forever, world without end. As the psalmist writes: "Lord, thou has been our dwelling place in all generations. Before the mountains were brought forth, or ever thou hadst formed the earth and the world, from everlasting to everlasting thou art God" (Ps 90:1–2). In the Letter to the Hebrews, the focus is on Jesus Christ as the creative Word of God in the beginning and the fulfilling Word of God in the ending. "Jesus Christ the same today, yesterday, and forever" (Heb 13:8). The Eucharistic liturgy joyfully responds after the transformation of the bread and wine, representing us and our world, into the body of Christ: "Christ has died. Christ is risen. Christ will come again." Past, present, future—all Christ—as it was in the beginning, is now, and will be forever, *world without end.* Amen.

In the ending as in the beginning the glory belongs to God. Creation itself "in its beginning," as we have seen above, remains a great mystery, but also a great gift. Creation "in its ending," world without end, remains a mystery as well, but likewise a great gift. The common understanding of the "last judgment," however, suggests fear of a God who will come to mete out reward and punishment. It is the time of God's justice, and one does not expect mercy in the last judgment. No one stands secure in such a judgment before God, and the "last judgment" seems dreadful with an unknown outcome to an unavoidable ordeal. Such is a common understanding and a misleading one.

Such misunderstanding was not prevalent among the early Christians who were yearning for the second coming of Jesus Christ and the end of time. "Amen. Come Lord Jesus!" (Rev 22:20) was a cry of jubilation that ended the Christian scriptures with an anticipation of rapture rather than distress. The lion of Judah who will come to judge our souls is as well the lamb of God who will wipe away our tears. The last day was awaited as the return of the beloved. The last judgment was a fulfillment of creation and not its peril. In the beginning, God saw all that God had created and said in the first judgment, "it is good." And when God has fulfilled all of creation in the fullness of time, when God has become at last "all in all" (1 Cor 15:28) in the ending, God will look upon all that has been created and graced and conclude in the last judgment: it was good, it is good, it will be forever very good, "world without end." Our God is a treasure hunter and not a garbage collector. No wonder Christians prayed "Come Lord

Jesus!" It would be the fullness of time and a world without end. "Though Jesus of Nazareth came in time and entered concretely into the human story enfleshing the Christ in history, Jesus *as* the Christ, is understood much more meaningfully as trans-historical, embracing in his salvific presence all of creation from the beginning to now and for all ages to come. In Christ Jesus, therefore, is the fullness of creation, the end of evolution, the eschaton."[63]

Judgment as fulfillment does justice to God's sovereignty. God has the whole world in his hands. God's providence is not trumped by human sinfulness. Paradoxically as it must appear to us, God is sovereign over human freedom and all the other causal events in the universe, whether they operate by chance or by physical law. God's sovereignty, however, sustains the very integrity of creation in all its manifestations. God does not undo human freedom by imposing himself from the outside. Human freedom has its very being within the sovereignty of God. Such is the mystery of God who is everything, while creating something out of nothing. What God has begun, God will finish. Whoever wills the end wills the means. God has intended all along to fulfill creation in a new heaven and new earth drawn into eternal life. Moreover, God is infinitely resourceful. We can presume that the communion of saints will enjoy the loving life of the Trinity. Jesus says in confidence "And this is the will of him who sent me, that I should lose nothing of all that he has given me, but raise it up on the last day" (Jn 6:39). In such hope Julian of Norwich says: "all shall be well and all manner of things shall be well."[64] God who created in the beginning will create in the ending.

One might thus imagine the last judgment as the last chapter of an intriguing story. Everything is resolved. All the pieces come together like parts of a jigsaw puzzle whose pattern is not revealed until the last piece is fitted into place. The judgment will explain the ways of God to men, and we will see, as did the disciples on the road to Emmaus "that the Messiah should suffer these things and then enter into his glory" (Lk 24:26). No tear will be wasted. Every thread of our life will belong to the pattern of this world's salvation. The last judgment will be a revelation of the finished story, the completed fabric. Working from the backside of a tapestry, the weaver cannot see the pattern nor understand why dark and bright colors are needed in just this way or that way. But viewed from the other side, when the work is done, and the finished tapestry is seen for the first time—then all its goodness is revealed, then every part belongs to every other part, then the fulfillment of all that labor in the dark is enjoyed forever. In the last judgment we will see what God has done, how God has done everything well, even while we in our freedom danced within the embrace of God's grace always and everywhere.

In his novel, *Brothers Karamatzov,* Dostoyevsky tells a poignant story in which the judgment of God is not imposed. God does nothing to condemn. The woman under judgment is revealed to herself, and she is her own judge. Let me retell the story. A woman who has died finds herself in hell, and in torment appeals to St. Peter for help. He in turn pleads with her to recall one example of something good she once did in her lifetime. She allows that once upon a time she gave a rotten onion to a beggar. St. Peter says that in God's mercy that is enough. He lowers the rotten onion into hell and the old woman grabs hold. She is pulled out of hell by clinging to the rotting onion that appears to be breaking away at any moment. Then someone else in hell takes hold of her ankles as she ascends. St. Peter continues to raise them both. Another takes hold, and a chain of human beings continues to be lifted out of hell. The woman is clinging to the frail onion. When she notices the others clinging to her feet, however, she kicks them off her ankles and the chain of people falls back. Then, and only then, does the onion snap. The woman herself falls back, for her heart is revealed and there is no love within her.[65] God does not condemn her. She judges herself. And love as Jesus loves would have been enough to raise them all.

A contemporary story suggests judgment is not imposed by God. The man in question is revealed to himself, and he remains his own judge. Judgment is not punishment from the outside but revelation from the inside. A young man is invited to an evening party. He wears a dark blue jacket, and when he steps into the party room, the "black light" that intended to create an atmosphere of festivity reveals all the dandruff on his shoulders. Like snowflakes they shine in the light for everyone to see. He is embarrassed, turns on his heels, and runs away. Note that no one asks him to leave. No one says that we do not accept people here with dandruff. No one says he is unclean. He judges that others would surely reject him, for were he in their place, he would condemn them. And so he condemns himself. Judgment becomes revelation of what we have become in our hearts.

Perhaps we might well conclude this reflection upon the judgment of God to come and the "world without end" with the story of Thomas, the disciple of Jesus who will not believe in the resurrection of the Lord "unless I see the mark of the nails in his hands, and put my finger in the mark of the nails and my hand in his side" (Jn 20:25). Seeing is believing, but touching is even more believing. Thomas does not believe crucifixion in this world will end in the resurrection of the body and life everlasting. When Jesus had earlier appeared to the gathered disciples, Thomas had been absent. He was alone, and alone we do not come to faith. Faith is born in us by the witness and the love of others. We are born in the Church, and we need to receive our spiritual life from the human community, just as we need to receive our physical life from our family. Once enfolded again in the disciples gathered together, Thomas is invited by Jesus to "put your finger here and see my hands. Reach out your hand and put it in my side" (Jn 20:27). Moved to belief by the willing disclosure of Jesus, Thomas foregoes his doubts, which must now seem the concomitant of isolation and insecurity. Heart speaks to heart. And Thomas exclaims, "my Lord and my God!" (Jn 20:28). Alone we do not embrace the grace of God. Hence the fullness of the resurrection of the body will not be complete until the last day when the fullness of the Church, the communion of saints, is achieved. Our life depends on one another, and we are not fulfilled until all of us are fulfilled in God's eternal life.

In the doubting Thomas story, one might notice that Thomas insists on seeing the wounds of Jesus. He wants to be sure the sufferings of the cross were not wasted as mere means to an end. Pain is not just an arbitrary detail of the Calvary story. The wounds of Jesus lie at the heart of the resurrection event, which Thomas is finding so difficult to believe. Our scars mark the wounds of our life. A baby is identifiable in the womb with the same fingerprints (skin scars of a sort) as it will possess as identifying markings all its life. People are known by their scars, physical and psychological, for each hurtful event was unique and left its own peculiar and indelible imprint. Our history is in our wounds, and perhaps the unseen wounds of the heart all the more. We do not just have a body; we belong to our body. And that body went through time and space with all the "slings and arrows of outrageous fortune that mortal flesh is heir to."[66] Thomas would put his finger in the nail wounds and his hand into the spear-pierced side of Jesus. He would touch the wounds in the body, and then without doubt he recognizes his Lord and his God.

In the resurrection appearances, the wounds of Jesus are shown to the disciples as proof of the identity of Jesus and the physicality of his body. A ghost or apparition would not have wounds. Jesus says to his disciples "'Look at my hands and my feet; see that it is I myself. Touch me and see; for a ghost does not have flesh and bones as you see that I have.' And when he had said this, he showed them his hands and his feet" (Lk 24:39–40). Pictorial representation of the wounds of Jesus shows them as wounds bathed in light. His wounds are healed and transfigured into glorious wounds, just as his body is healed from death and rises in full glory from the tomb. The glory of God is light in contrast to the darkness of the tomb and death. Jesus forever shines and his body glows with light as on the Tabor mountain, when "he was transfigured before them, and his face shone like the sun, and his clothes became dazzling white" (Mt 17:2).

The Thomas story ends with an appeal to faith that now touches Jesus with the heart and need not touch him with hands in order to believe. "Blessed are those who have not seen and yet have come to believe" (Jn 20:29). Those words are addressed to us who come after the resurrection appearances of Jesus recounted in the scriptures. In our doubts we too may see the wounds of this life as diminishments and anything but glorious. We may fear that our body is in jeopardy and that we may be hurt. We may wonder if a "world without end" can ever be or can ever make all things and events come round right. And as ever in matters of total trust, "whoever does not receive the kingdom of God as a little child will never enter it" (Mk 10:15).

The implications of the glorious wounds of Jesus must not be missed. When we send a satellite into space, the rocket booster that lifts the cargo out of earth's atmosphere falls away, spent and expendable. We may think that our body exists only to lift our souls into eternity, and then our body is discarded, unneeded and unwanted in the heavenly life. We may think the history of our lives and of this our earthly hope is but a means to an end. You cannot take it with you, and you are well rid of the bodiliness of the human condition anyway. But that kind of thinking is not Christianity. We believe in the resurrection of the body and life everlasting. This body will live forever. This world made glorious as "a new heaven and a new earth" (Rev 21:1) will live in glory forever. The "world without end," imprecise as the translation of the original Greek and subsequent Latin may be, holds the truth plainly before our eyes. Nothing of creation is to be lost, nothing wasted. The incarnation of Jesus made the matter of his body and the extended matter of this world to matter forever before God. The body (this material world of time and space) is to enjoy communion with God. The world is not to dead end. The world in its transfiguration is to become heaven. In the resurrection of Jesus, we see in anticipation the assumption of the flesh into the heart of God. Glorious in his woundedness, he is seated in body at the right hand of the Father. And when we pray our doxologies, we give glory to these many glories of God, and we say in effect over and over again with Thomas our words of wonder: "my Lord and my God," our Lord and our God, "as it was in the beginning, is now, and shall be forever, world without end. Amen."

"Amen"

The Book of Revelation ends with these lines: "'Surely, I am coming soon.' Amen. Come, Lord Jesus! The grace of the Lord Jesus
be with all" (Rev 22:20 – 21). *Amen* is a Semitic word that means
"thus" or "it is true." *Amen* is rooted in the verb *mn*, which is related to various Hebrew words indicating truth, faith, and trust.[67]
In saying Amen one is saying "yes" to all of life in the providence
of God, who is sovereign Lord of all that comes about. Paul writes:
"For the Son of God, Jesus Christ, whom we proclaimed among
you, Silvanus and Timothy and I, was not 'Yes and No'; but in
him it is always 'Yes.' For in him every one of God's promises is
a 'Yes.' For this reason it is through him that we say the 'Amen,'
to the glory of God. But it is God who establishes us with you in
Christ and has anointed us, by putting his seal on us and giving
us his Spirit in our hearts as a first installment" (2 Cor 1:19 – 22).
Thus, at the end of a prayer led by another, the Amen signifies
that the respondent accepts the prayer as his or her own, approves
its sentiments, and concurs in its petition. "So be it" in English
(*Ainsi soit-il* in French or *Così sia* in Italian) captures something

of the content of Amen. Justin Martyr writes in the second century: "At the end of these prayers [Eucharistic prayers] and thanksgiving, all present express their approval by saying 'Amen'. This Hebrew word, 'Amen,' means 'So be it.'"[68] St. Augustine writes of the word "Amen" in one of his sermons: "My brethren, your Amen is your signature; it is your consent; it is your confirmation."[69] The word "Amen" is so ancient and venerable in Jewish and Christian prayer that it hardly requires a translation. One commentator writes that the Amen was "understood as the ratification of any blessing" and at the conclusion of prayers it was understood as "the appropriation of the intent which had been expressed, and thus, functioned as an affirming doxology for worshippers."[70]

A Last Word

"God for us is who God is as God."[1] As Jesus said: "Whoever has seen me has seen the Father" (1 Jn 14:9). Shaped by the doctrinal controversies of early Christianity, the first part of the Gloria Patri names the Trinity with no commentary but with the "glory" standing for the very being of God, whereas the second part of the doxology proclaims the trinity of persons as ever and forever. Paul writes that "in Christ we have also obtained an inheritance, having been destined according to the purpose of him who accomplishes all things according to his counsel and will, so that we, who were the first to set our hope on Christ, might live for the praise of his glory" (Eph 1:11–12). Indeed, for Paul "the sum and substance of the Christian life is to live for the praise of God's glory."[2]

That glory no "eye has seen, nor ear heard, nor the human heart conceived, what God has prepared for those who love him" (1 Cor 2:9). We cannot imagine God in God's own infinite being. Creation from nothing is so easily reduced to the miraculous unfoldings of an evolution beyond the scale of our imagination, rather than the mysterious self-sharing of an infinite God. In-carnation of the Son of God made flesh is so easily reduced to a miraculous baby born without an earthly father, rather than the mystery of the uncreated God become human with us. Resurrection of the crucified Jesus is so easily reduced to the reanimation of a "Lazarus" who will die again, rather than the mystery of un-created eternity overcoming all human death in time. The Eucharistic bread is so easily reduced to a miraculous change of substance, water into wine, rather than the uncreated mystery of the real presence of Jesus in the matter, the words, and the people of this earth forever taken up into the mystery of God. Doxology reaches even for the uncreated glory of God—Father, Son, and Holy Spirit—beyond God's reflection in our created world. The glory of God is never only the glory of this world risen to the heights. The glory of God remains the glory beyond, the glory back before back, the glory where nowhere, the glory when no-ever, the glory of gift and giver all one, "as it was in the beginning, is now, and ever shall be, world without end."

A Poem of Glory

Our bodies
Our minds
Our hearts
Our souls
       Merging
       Mingling
       Growing
       ever closer
       ever deeper
Unfolding and flowing into that one love
The only love
The love the Father, Son, and Holy Spirit share
                   "That they may be one as we are one"
       Merging
       Mingling
       Growing
       ever closer
       ever deeper
       Day unto day
       Night unto night

With the rhythm of creation
Through and in the fullness of our humanity
In the dignity of our divinity
        Merging
        Mingling
        Growing
        ever closer
        ever deeper
        Day unto day
        Night unto night
        Touching . . . tasting
        Hearing . . . seeing
        Experiencing
        Knowing
Now . . . in time . . . that which is timeless
        GLORY
The Glory of ETERNAL LOVE
                ETERNAL GOD
           GLORY . . . LOVE . . . GOD . . . US
All One . . . All God . . . All Us . . . All Love
        OUR GLORY   GOD'S GLORY

by Susan Pusztai

Notes

Preface

1. The "Glory to God in the Highest" recited in the Eucharistic liturgy is a longer and more elaborate doxological prayer, and hence has been widely named the "greater doxology."

2. The saying *lex orandi, lex credendi* is a shortened form of the original quotation of Prosper of Aquitaine, *legem credendi lex statuat supplicandi* (the rule of praying determines the rule of believing). Cf. Catherine Mowry LaCugna, *God For Us: The Trinity and Christian Life* (San Francisco: Harper, 1991), 112.

Part One

1. All biblical citations are taken from the New Revised Standard Version.

2. See, for example, the homilies of Pope Leo the Great.

3. The original version of the Gloria was a Greek Christian hymn, possibly composed in the fourth century. It is still used in the Byzantine Orthodox "Morning Prayer."

4. "The Martyrdom of Saint Polycarp," trans. Francis Glimm, in *The Apostolic Fathers,* The Fathers of the Church (New York: Cima Publishing Co., 1947), 158.

5. "Canon Three," in *The Canons of Hippolytus,* ed. Paul Bradshaw, trans. Carol Bebawi (Bramcote Nottingham: Grove Books, 1987), 13.

6. Origen, "On Prayer," in *Alexandrian Christianity: Selected Translations of Clement and Origen,* The Library of Christian Classics 2 (Philadelphia: Westminster Press, 1954), chap. 33, paragraph 6.

7. Clement of Alexandria, *Quis dives salutem consequi possit* (London: Ogles, Duncan, and Cochrane, 1816).

8. Joseph Jungmann, *The Place of Christ in Liturgical Prayer,* trans. A. Peeler, 2nd rev. ed. (New York: Alba House, 1965), 194.

9. The beauty and glory of God and the "guiding concept of glory" is the focus of Hans Urs Von Balthasar's *The Glory of the Lord: A Theological Aesthetics,* 7 vols. (repr., San Francisco: Ignatius Press, 1989).

10. At the same time, dictionaries dictate usage. In a marvelous back and forth, dictionaries are created by usage and in turn modify language according to their definitions and their record of changing usage.

11. Cf. Balthasar, *Glory of the Lord,* 6:31–37. When paired with a following word, the first vowel in *kabod* is reduced. Hence *kebod Yahveh.*

12. A. J. Vermeulen, *The Semantic Development of Gloria in Early-Christian Latin,* Latinitas Christianorum Primavera 12 (Nijmegen: Dekker and van de Vegt, 1956), 11.

13. Vermeulen, *Semantic Development of Gloria,* 11.

14. Vermeulen, *Semantic Development of Gloria,* 12 and n. 1.

15. Cf. Christine Mohrmann, "Epiphania," *Revue des Sciences Philosophiques et Théologiques* 37 (1953): 644–70.

16. See Balthasar, *Glory of the Lord,* 7:239–44.

17. For example, see the prologue of the Gospel of John: "In the beginning was the Word, and the Word was with God, and the Word was God" (Jn 1:1).

18. Mohrmann, "Epiphania."

19. C. S. Lewis, *The Weight of Glory and other Addresses,* ed. Walter Hooper (New York: Macmillan, 1949), 13.

20. André Laurentin, *Dóxa: Etude des Commentaires de Jean 17:5 depuis les origines jusqu'a S. Thomas d'Aquin,* 3 vols. (Paris: Bloud and Gay, 1972). See especially "Evolution de la Notion de la Gloire," 1:220–53.

21. Vermeulen, *Semantic Development of Gloria,* 18. See also "Gloria in the Latin Versions of the Bible," 5–27, and "Concluding Remarks," 221–30.

22. *New Dictionary of Sacramental Worship,* ed. Peter E. Fink (Collegeville, MN: Liturgical Press, 1990), s. v. "Holy Spirit in Christian Worship."

23. Edgar Allen Poe, "To Helen."

24. Cicero, "De Inventione," book 2, paragraph 55.

25. Saint Augustine, "Contra Maximum Episcopum Arianorum," in *Patrologiae Cursus Completus,* Series Latina, ed. J.-P. Migne (Paris: Garnieri Fratres, 1844–55), 42:770.

26. Augustine's *clara cum laude notitia* suggests Jesus as the glory that reveals God as Trinity: *soli sapienti Deo gloria sit per Jesum Christum, hoc est, clara cum laude notitia qua innotuit gentibus Deum Trinitas.* Ibid.

27. Vermeulen, *Semantic Development of Gloria,* 174.

28. Lewis, *Weight of Glory,* 19.

29. Ibid., 17.

30. Irenaeus, *Adversus Haereses,* book 4, section 20, paragraph 7.

31. Geoffrey Wainwright, *Eucharist and Eschatology* (New York: Oxford University Press, 1981), 103.

32. Excerpt from T. S. Eliot, "Little Gidding" from the *Four Quartets,* in *Collected Poems 1909-1962* (New York: Harcourt, Brace & Company, 1936).

33. Saint Basil, *On the Holy Spirit,* trans. David Anderson (Crestwood, NY: St. Vladimir's Seminary Press, 1980). Saint Basil the Great (c. 329–79) was from Caesarea in Cappadocia (modern-day northern Turkey).

34. Basil, *On the Holy Spirit,* paragraph 77.

35. The Syriac language in contrast with the Greek language provides no other conjunctions besides and/and for the doxology. See Catherine Mowry LaCugna, *God For Us: The Trinity and Christian Life* (San Francisco: Harper, 1991), 121.

36. Basil, *On the Holy Spirit,* paragraph 68.

37. Herbert Thurston, "Notes on Familiar Prayers," *The Month* 131 (May, 1918): 406.

38. Cassian, "De Coenobiorum Institutione," Book II, Chapter VIII in Migne, *Patrologiae,* 49:94.

39. See chapters 13 and 18.

40. J. D. Mansi, *Sacrorum Conciliorum Nova et Amplissima Collectio,* 58 vols. (Paris: H. Welter, 1901–27), 8:727.

41. Jean Hardouin, *Acta Conciliorum et Epistolae Decretales, ac Constitutiones Summorum Pontificum,* 12 vols. (Paris: Typographia Regia, 1714–15), tome III, col. 575, canon XV.

42. Walahfrid Strabo, *Libellus de Exordiis et Incrementis Quarundam in Observationibus Ecclesiasticis Rerum,* trans. and commentary by Alice L. Harting-Correa (Leiden: Brill, 1996), paragraph XXVI, pp. 162–63.

43. Thurston, "Notes on Familiar Prayers," 414 (translation mine). The Mozarabic liturgy was to all effects abolished by the Gregorian Reform of the eleventh century.

44. R. G. Davis, letter to the editor, *The Tablet* 97 (1901): 257.

45. H. G., letter to the editor, *The Tablet* 64 (1884): 500, reprinting a letter of Dr. John Lingard to the *Catholic Magazine* (1833): 133.

46. From a fourteenth-century primer found in William Maskill, *Monumenta Ritualia* [1st ed., 1846], 2:xxxiv and 2:3, cited in A. N., letter to the editor, *The Tablet* 122 (1913): 183.

47. John Dowden, *The Workmanship of the Prayer Book* (London: Methuen, 1899), 167.

48. Ibid.

49. From a sixteenth-century Primer of the Church of Rome, cited in H. S. B., letter to the editor, *The Tablet* 122 (1913): 224.

50. John Lingard, *Manual of Prayers on Sunday and during Mass* (1833 and 1837), 6, cited in R. N. B., letter to the editor, *The Tablet* 97 (1901): 416.

51. G. S., letter to the editor, *The Tablet* 97 (1901): 335.

52. Vermeulen, *Semantic Development of Gloria,* 174–75. Ambrose was engaged in long controversy with the Arians, who had the sympathy of the Emperor's wife.

53. Jungmann, *Place of Christ,* 188.

54. M. F. H., letter to the editor, *The Tablet* 97 (1901): 495.

55. *Praying Together* was authored by the English Language Liturgical Consultation (ELLC), which is a successor of ICET and which undertakes a liturgical mission wider than establishing texts alone.

56. Cited in Thurston, "Notes on Familiar Prayers," 412n.2.

57. William Maskell, *Monumenta Ritualia* [2nd ed., 1882], 1:ccxli [n. 13], cited in Charles Boardman, letter to the editor, *The Tablet* 64 (1884): 339.

58. William Maskell, *Monumenta Ritualia* [2nd ed., 1882], 3:6, cited in Charles Boardman, letter to the editor, *The Tablet* 64 (1884): 339.

59. Thurston, "Notes on Familiar Prayers," 411.

60. Jungmann, *Place of Christ,* 200.

61. The argument for *sicut erat* as a parenthesis is convincingly made in F. E. Brightman's classic study, *The English Rite: Being a Synopsis of the Sources and Revisions of the Book of Common Prayer,* 2 vols. (London: Rivingtons, 1915), p. 1:lxvii.

62. In the Latin, the first part of the doxology is dactyllic with fifteen syllables, and the second part is mainly anapestic, also with fifteen syllables. In the English the first part is dactyllic with eighteen syllables, and the second part is mainly anapestic, with seventeen syllables if "unto ages of ages" is employed in a literal translation of the Greek and of the Latin.

Part Two

1. Catherine LaCugna's book, *God For Us: The Trinity and Christian Life* (San Francisco: Harper, 1991), has been a major source of my explanation throughout, and while her thought echoes that of earlier theologians of the twentieth century, she develops the implications with a thoroughness and spirituality that makes the thesis truly her own. David Cunningham's, *These Three are One: The Practice of Trinitarian Theology* (Oxford: Blackwell, 1998), which explores the many implications of Trinitarian doctrine for actual Christian living, gives a helpful overview; see especially his annotated bibliography, 339–42.

2. John Paul II, "Tertio Millennio Adveniente" (Apostolic Letter, Nov. 10, 1994), paragraph 44.

3. LaCugna, *God For Us,* 305.

4. Ibid., 231.

5. Allusion to the Trinity has also been noted by some believers in many places of the Pauline Christian scriptures, such as 1 Cor 6:11, 1 Cor 12:4–5, 2 Cor 1:21–22, 1 Th 5:18–19, Gal 3:11–14, 1 Pt 1:2, Heb 10:29.

6. LaCugna, *God For Us,* 351,

7. Ibid., 320.

8. John Paul II, "Tertio Millennio Adveniente," paragraph 55; italics in original.

9. Ibid., paragraph 56; italics in original.

10. John Paul II, *God, Father and Creator* (Boston: Pauline Books, 1996), 211.

11. LaCugna, *God For Us,* 228; italics in original.

12. Ibid., 296.

13. John Paul II, "Tertio Millennio Adveniente," paragraph 45.

14. T. E. Lawrence, *Seven Pillars of Wisdom* (Harmondsworth: Penguin, 1971), 364, quoted and discussed in John Dunne, *The Reasons of the Heart* (New York: Macmillan), 1–3.

15. LaCugna, *God For Us,* 398.

16. Aidan Kavanagh, *On Liturgical Theology* (New York: Pueblo, 1984).

17. LaCugna, *God For Us,* 381.

18. Thomas Torrance, *The Christian Doctrine of God: One Being Three Persons* (Edinburgh: T. T. Clark, 1996), 202.

19. LaCugna, *God For Us,* 352.

20. Sebastian Moore, *Let this Mind Be in You* (Minneapolis: Winston, 1985), 23.

21. Richard Downs, C.S.C., "The Trinity and the Indwelling of Christian Friendship" (unpublished manuscipt).

22. Ibid.

23. Ibid.

24. David Cunningham, *These Three Are One: The Practice of Trinitarian Theology.* (Oxford: Blackwell, 1998), 8.

25. Hans Urs Von Balthasar, in his book *Love Alone* (New York: Herder and Herder, 1969), speaks well of "God's own love, the manifestation of which is the manifestation of the glory of God." He changes the Jesuit motto, *ad majorem Dei gloriam* to *ad majorem Divini Amoris gloriam.*

26. Downs, "Trinity."

27. Ibid.

28. LaCugna, *God For Us,* 383.

29. Downs, "Trinity."

30. Ibid.

31. LaCugna, *God For Us,* 409.

32. See Mary Daly, *Beyond God the Father* (Boston: Beacon Press, 1973).

33. See Cunningham, *These Three are One,* which refers to Sallie McFague's *Models of God* (Philadelphia: Fortress Press, 1987). McFague lists some possible alternatives to the traditional Trinitarian language, such as, mother, lover, friend; source, well spring, living water; author,

primary actor, director; creator, redeemer, sanctifier. Cunningham also points out Augustine's metaphors for the Trinity, such as, lover, beloved, love; mind, knowledge, love; memory, understanding, will. See Cunningham, 73–74. See also Thomas Marsh, *The Triune God,* 28–31 and 186–90, which also raises the issue of gender language with reference to the Trinity.

34. LaCugna, *God For Us,* 354; italics in original.

35. Augustine, *Confessions,* trans. Henry Chadwick (New York: Oxford University Press, 1991), book 11, paragraph 13, 229–30.

36. Catherine Pickstock, *After Writing: On the Liturgical Consummation of Philosophy.* (Oxford: Blackwell, 1997) 204.

37. *The Trial of Joan of Arc: Being the Verbatim Report of the Proceedings from the Orleans Manuscript,* trans. W. S. Scott (London: Folio Society, 1956), 73.

38. The six blessings of Eph 1:1–14 (to live through God's love; to be God's adopted children; to be destined to praise the glory of God's grace; to be redeemed; to know the revelation of the mystery of salvation; to be the chosen Jewish race; to be as pagans included in the chosen race by the gift of the Holy Spirit) have been "compared to the beginning of the Eighteen Benedictions (*Shemoneh Esreh*) employed in late-1st century AD Jewish synagogue worship" in Raymond Brown, *An Introduction to the New Testament* (New York: Doubleday, 1997), 622n.4. Notice that benedictions dovetail easily with doxology.

39. Advent antiphon for First Vespers, Fourth Sunday of Advent.

40. Intercessions from the First Vespers, Third Sunday of Advent.

41. Antiphon at the Canticle of Zachary, Epiphany Morning Prayer.

42. See Christine Mohrmann, "Epiphania," *Revue des Sciences Philosophiques et Théologiques* 37 (1953): 644–70.

43. Soren Kierkegaard, *Philosophical Fragments,* ed. and trans. Howard Hong and Edna Hong (Princeton: Princeton University Press, 1985), 26–28.

44. Attributed to George MacDonald.

45. The homily of Leo the Great in the Office of Readings in the *Divine Office* for Christmas day.

46. See also Ex 13:21, 16:10, and Dt 31:15.

47. *The Roman Missal.*

48. John Paul II, "Dies Domini," (Apostolic Letter, July 5, 1998), paragraph 75.

49. See Edward Schillebeeckx, *Christ the Sacrament of Encounter with God* (New York: Sheed and Ward, 1965).

50. Karl Rahner, "Worship," in *Theological Investigations,* vol 19, trans. Edward Quinn (New York: Crossroad, 1983), 146; emphasis mine.

51. Aidan Kavanagh in *On Liturgical Theology* makes a similar distinction between liturgy "about God" (Rahner's "in the world") and liturgy "of God."

52. Rahner, "Worship," 149.

53. This understanding of sacrament comes from an address by Michael Himes.

54. J. R. R. Tolkien, *The Two Towers,* in *The Lord of the Rings,* collectors ed. (Boston: Houghton, Mifflin, 1987), book 2, "Farewell to Lorien," 385–86.

55. Pierre Teilhard de Chardin, "The Mass on the World," in *Hymn of the Universe,* trans. Willian Collins and Sons Co. (New York: Harper and Row, 1965), 23.

56. Antiphon at the Magnificat, Vespers of *Corpus Christi.*

57. Geoffrey Wainwright, *Doxology: The Praise of God in Worship, Doctrine, and Life; A Systematic Theology,* (New York: Oxford University Press, 1980), 352.

58. "World of worlds" would be a literal translation of the Latin (*in saecula saeculorum*), which follows closely the Greek. "World without end" does capture the meaning of always, as does my own translation of the doxology: "as in the beginning, so now and always, *forever and ever.*" See the discussion in the chapter above titled "the History of the Gloria Patri Doxology."

59. Gerard Manley Hopkins, *Poems of Gerard Manley Hopkins* (London: Oxford University Press, 1930; orig. pub. London: H. Milford, 1918), 26.

60. John Paul II, "Dies Domini," paragraph 18.

61. Ibid., paragraph 84.

62. St. Basil, *On the Holy Spirit,* trans. David Anderson (Crestwood, NY: St. Vladimir's Seminary Press, 1980), paragraph 101.

63. Barbara Fiand, *Embraced by Compassion* (New York: Crossroad, 1993), 119.

64. Julian of Norwich, *Revelations of Divine Love* (London: Methuen, 1949), 56.

65. Fyodor Dostoyevsky, *Brothers Karamatzov* (New York: Heritage Press, 1949), part 3, book 7, chapter 3, 271.

66. Shakespeare, "Hamlet," 3.1.57.

67. Much of this paragraph was taken from my own book, *The Hail Mary: A Verbal Icon of Mary* (Notre Dame, IN: University of Notre Dame Press, 1994), 124–25.

68. Justin Martyr, "The First Apology," in *Saint Justin Martyr: The Fathers of the Church,* trans. Thomas Falls (New York: Christian Heritage, 1948), chap. 65, p. 105.

69. Saint Augustine, a sermon against the Pelagians, in *Patrologiae Cursus Completus,* Series Latina, ed. J.-P. Migne (Paris: Garnieri Fratres, 1844–55), 39:1721.

70. *New Dictionary of Sacramental Worship,* ed. Peter E. Fink (Collegeville, MN: Liturgical Press, 1990), s.v. "Doxology."

A Last Word

1. Catherine LaCugna, *God For Us: The Trinity and Christian Life* (San Francisco: Harper, 1991), 305.

2. LaCugna, 377.

Select Bibliography

Abrahams, Israel. *The Glory of God.* London: Oxford University Press, 1925.

Balthasar, Hans Urs Von. *The Glory of the Lord: A Theological Aesthetics.* 7 vols. Trans. Erasmo Leiva-Merikakis, ed. Joseph Fession and John Riches. San Francisco: Ignatius Press, 1983.

———. *Love Alone.* Trans. and ed. Alexander Dru. New York: Herder and Herder, 1969.

Basil the Great, Saint. *On the Holy Spirit.* Crestwood, NY: St. Vladimir's Seminary Press, 1980.

Catholic Dictionary of Theology. London: Nelson, 1967. S.v. "doxology."

Catholic Encyclopedia. New York: Universal Knowledge Foundation, 1909. S.v. "doxology."

Cunningham, David. *These Three Are One: The Practice of Trinitarian Theology.* Oxford: Blackwell, 1998.

Dictionary of Christian Antiquities. Ed. William Smith and Samuel Cheetham. London: John Murray, 1875. S.v. "doxology."

Dictionnaire d'Archéologie Chrétienne et de Liturgie. Paris: Librairie Letouzey et Ane, 1921. S.v. "doxologies."

Dictionnaire de Théologie Catholique. Paris: Letouzey et Ané, 1923–50. S.v. "gloire."

Dowden, John. *The Workmanship of the Prayer Book in Its Literary and Liturgical Aspects.* London: Methuen, 1899.

Jungmann, Joseph. *The Mass of the Roman Rite: Its Origins and Development.* 2 vols. Trans. Francis Brunner. New York: Benziger, 1950.

———. *The Place of Christ in Liturgical Prayer.* 2d. rev. ed. Trans. A. Peeler. New York: Alba House, 1965.

Kavanagh, Aidan. *On Liturgical Theology.* New York: Pueblo, 1984.

LaCugna, Catherine. *God For Us: The Trinity and Christian Life.* San Francisco: Harper, 1991.

Lauentin, André. *Dóxa: Étude des Commentaires de Jean 17:5 depuis les origines jusqu'à S. Thomas d'Aquin.* 3 vols. Paris: Bloud and Gay, 1972.

Lebreton, Jules. *Histoire du Dogme de la Trinité: Des Origines à Saint Augustin.* 2 vols. Paris: Gabriel Beauchesne, 1928.

———. *Les Origines du Dogme de la Trinité.* Paris: Gabriel Beauchesne, 1919. See "doxologies," 330–32.

Lewis, C. S. *The Weight of Glory and Other Addresses.* Ed. Walter Hooper. New York: Macmillan, 1949.

Lexikon für Theologie und Kirke. Freiburg: Herder, 1959. S.v. "dóxa."

Marsh, Thomas. *The Triune God: A Biblical, Historical, and Theological Study.* Dublin: Columba Press, 1994.

Maskell, William. *Documenta Ecclesiae Anglicanae: The Occasional Office of the Church of England according to the Old Use of Salisbury the Prymer in English and Other Prayers and Forms, with Dissertations and Notes.* 3 vols. Oxford: Clarendon Press, 1882.

Modern Concordance to the New Testament. Ed. Michael Darton. New York: Doubleday, 1976. S.v. "doxa."

Pass, H. Leonard. *The Glory of the Father: A Study in St. John XIII-XVII.* London: A. R. Mowbray, 1935.

Pickstock, Catherine. *After Writing: On the Liturgical Consummation of Philosophy.* Oxford: Blackwell, 1997.

Prayer Book Dictionary. Ed. George Harford and Morley Stevenson. New York: Isaac Pitman and Sons, 1925. S.v. "doxology."

Selwyn, E. G. "The Father's Glory." *Theology* 24 (1932): 142–56.

Sieben, Herman Josef. *Voces.* Berlin: Walter De Gruyter, 1980. S.vv. "doxa" and "gloria."

Teilhard de Chardin, Pierre. *The Divine Milieu.* Trans. Bernard Wall. New York: Harper and Brothers, 1960.

———. "The Mass on the World," in *Hymn of the Universe*. Trans. William Collins and Sons Co. New York: Harper and Row, 1965.

Torrance, Alan. *Persons in Communion: An Essay on Trinitarian Description and Human Participation.* Edinburgh: T. T. Clark, 1996.

Torrance, Thomas. *The Christian Doctrine of God: One Being Three Persons.* Edinburgh: T. T. Clark, 1996.

Thurston, Herbert. "Notes on Familiar Prayers: The 'Gloria Patri.'" *The Month* 131 (May 1918): 406–17.

Vermeulen, A. J. *The Semantic Development of Gloria in Early-Christian Latin.* Latinitas Christianorum Primaeva 12. Nijmegen: Dekker and Van de Vegt, 1956.

Wainwright, Geoffrey. *Doxology: The Praise of God in Worship, Doctrine, and Life; A Systematic Theology.* New York: Oxford University Press, 1980.

———. *Eucharist and Eschatology.* New York: Oxford University Press, 1981.

Weinandy, Thomas. *Does God Suffer?* Notre Dame, IN: University of Notre Dame Press, 2000.